A Personal Approach To Teaching

Beliefs That Make A Difference

Arthur W. Combs

Distinguished Professor
University of Northern Colorado

Allyn and Bacon, Inc.

Boston   London   Sydney   Toronto

Library of Congress Cataloging in Publication Data

Combs, Arthur Wright.
 A personal approach to teaching.

 Includes bibliographical references and index.
 1. Teaching. 2. Educational psychology. I. Title.
LB1025.2.C628   371.1'02   81-10788
ISBN 0-205-07643-2 (pbk.)   AACR2

Printed in the United States of America.

10 9 8 7 6 5 4 3 2   91 90 89 88 87 86

Contents

Preface

Curriculum workers and teacher educators have often lamented the lack of an adequate theory of teaching. Now and then some hardy soul has attempted to construct such a theory, but to this point those efforts have proven to be most disappointing. One reason it is so difficult to develop a comprehensive theory of teaching is the fact that education is not a basic science. It is an applied field of endeavor in which workers apply appropriate principles from such basic disciplines as psychology, sociology, philosophy, biology, or anthropology. Theory construction is difficult enough in a basic science. It is almost impossible in an applied profession that draws its basic premises from many different sources.[1]

A second reason it is difficult to design a comprehensive theory of teaching is the fact that teaching is a highly individual matter. Research on good teaching has been unable to establish any specific knowledge, method, or behavior clearly and reliably associated with either good teaching or bad. Instead, teaching seems to be a highly personal matter having to do with the ways in which individual teachers use themselves and their skills to carry out their own and society's purposes. How teachers use themselves, in turn, is determined by the personal system of beliefs from which they make their choices. Thus, teacher belief systems serve as individual theories of teaching and provide a personal set of guidelines for professional practice.

Each person in the process of becoming a teacher constructs a personal theory that guides his or her choice of goals, methods, strategies, or behavior for carrying out the teaching task. Some of these beliefs are adopted from science or research. Some are acquired from experience or learned from other people. Some are held in common with other educators and some are totally unique, existing for a particular teacher and no one else. While it is not possible to develop a single theory applicable to everyone in the profession, individual teachers can and do develop their own theories of teaching. It is also possible to refine and improve one's personal theories, so that they become more effective and satisfying guides for professional thought and action. That is what this book is about.

In Chapter 1, I have tried to outline the concept of a personal theory for teaching and why it is important. Following that, I have set down what I believe are essential criteria for a sufficient personal theory. The chapter ends with a discussion of ways in which theories come into being and how one's personal system of beliefs can be refined and improved. In the remainder of the book, I have outlined, in simple fashion, the major aspects of the personal theory of teaching I have acquired in the course of a long career and tried to show significant ways in which it has affected my professional thinking and practice.

No one, of course, can *give* another a personal theory of teaching. Each teacher develops his or her own. But one of the important ways in which persons can refine their own beliefs is by confronting the beliefs of others. I have therefore presumed to present my personal theory of teaching here for at least the following reasons:

1   The first reason is a very personal one. Writing is a creative experience for me. I value the opportunities provided by its discipline to explore and order my thinking. I have therefore tried to state my personal theory of teaching as it stands at this moment in the hope of refining and clarifying it further.

2   This book allows one to see what a personal theory and its implications for practice look like in print for, so far as I know, no one has ever looked at matters in quite this way before.

3   My personal theory of teaching is the present expression of a life-long distillation of experience and study, first, as a human being and, after that, as teacher, counselor, school psychologist, consultant, administrator, writer, educational psychologist, and designer of a successful program of teacher education. I have wrestled with it, poked it, questioned it, and tested it in hundreds of ways. In the process I have come to trust it as a reliable guide for most of my interactions with other people both in and out of the classroom. It has served me well and, I believe, it meets the criteria for good theory outlined in Chapter 1. I have tried to set it down here in the hope that it may prove stimulating and helpful for others in the teaching profession as well.

Not all aspects of anyone's personal theory of teaching have relevance for others. Some of our beliefs are so very personal as to have no value for anyone else whatever. Still other facets are so specific that they apply only to particular times, places, persons, or circumstances. Because I want this book to have general appeal, I have included in this discussion only those aspects of my personal theory which seem to me to have broad significance for education.

I have tried in each chapter to state the gist of my personal theory, then to suggest some of the implications of such thinking for educational thought and practice. While I began my professional career as a junior and senior high school teacher, counselor and school psychologist, most of my latter years have been spent in colleges of education. Some of the implications of my theory naturally mirror that experience. Because my illustrations are frequently drawn from my college teaching experience, it should not be supposed the beliefs they are based upon are useful only for that level. Quite the contrary. I believe the concepts I have included here have relevance at all levels of education, including preschool, elementary, and secondary, and I have no doubt they would find expression in my teaching if I were employed at such levels. My colleagues who teach such classes also assure me the beliefs I have expressed do, indeed, have relevance for their levels as well. I believe a personal theory of teaching should be just that—personal. I have therefore made no attempt to suggest what could or should be done outside my areas of expertise. Let the reader, therefore, regard my illustrations as "Combs' attempts to implement his theory" and ask, "If those beliefs make sense, what then does it mean for thinking and practice at my place in the profession?"

I have made no attempt to document every aspect of the theory presented here. That has been done extensively in two of my other books, Helping Relationships and Perceptual Psychology.[2] Interested scholars will find in those books nearly a thousand references supporting the psychological basis upon which much of my personal theory rests. In this volume I have listed in the endnotes for each chapter only a few references of general significance.

In addition to the colleagues and students who have supported my work and stimulated my thinking over the years, I am especially indebted to: Donald Avila, Cile Chavez, Jerry Christian, Bonnie Clute, Frank Cordell, Kent Estes, Chuck Luna, Mary Jean Murdoch, and Richard Usher for critical reading of the manuscript and for many helpful suggestions. I am also appreciative of the help of Susan Kannel and Dorothy Rich in preparation of the manuscript for publication.

I have been a teacher for all but one year of my professional life. I have great faith in education and I have profited much from involvement in all its phases. My experience in teaching has contributed enormously to my growth and fulfillment, not just as a teacher, but as a person as well. I am deeply grateful to this noble institution and believe it to be the most significant of our helping professions. As an intimate member of the family, however, I am also sorely aware of its shortcomings, especially its slowness to respond to current needs of society and youth and to new conceptions of the nature of persons and the processes of learning. Perhaps this book may help to speed those needed adaptations. If so, I will rest content to have made some reciprocal contribution to the profession that has given so much to me.

CHAPTER 1

Why a Personal Theory of Teaching?

Once it was believed that a person who knew a subject was automatically able to teach it. The belief that knowledge of subject matter is the primary requisite for good teaching is still widely held. Unfortunately, mere knowledge of content provides no guarantee at all that instructors will be able to teach effectively. Almost everyone has, at one time or another, been exposed to teachers who knew their subjects but could not teach worth a hoot. Knowledge of subject matter by itself is clearly not enough to assure good teaching.

A second fallacy about good teaching is that it is a question of teacher behavior or methods. Operating on this assumption, educators and psychologists have tried repeatedly to define "the teaching act" or to catalog specific competencies and skills considered essential for good teaching. To this end they have carried out hundreds of studies on teacher behavior, methods, classroom organization, and teaching strategies with completely ambiguous results. From careful review of these researches one can only conclude that there is no teacher behavior or method of teaching that can be clearly shown to be a trustworthy indicator of either good or bad teaching.[1]

What an impasse! One cannot tell the difference between good teachers and poor ones on the basis of either knowledge or methods. Yet everyone knows from personal experience that there are good teachers and poor ones. What makes the difference?

THE PROBLEM-SOLVING NATURE OF HELPING PROFESSIONS

To make heads or tails of the disappointing character of the researches on teaching, it is necessary to understand the nature of a profession. What distinguishes a profession like counseling, social work, medicine, law, pastoral care, or teaching from more mechanical operations is the necessity for the professional worker to act as an instantaneous problem solver. All the helping professions require practitioners to respond instantaneously to events encountered in the course of practice. When the client says something, the counselor must respond. When a child asks a question, the teacher must reply. In the helping professions there are no cut and dried acts to perform, no precise words to say, and no correct methods to be applied in given situations. Professional workers must invent responses on the spot.

This explains why we are unable to find specific methods regularly associated with good or bad teaching. The teacher's process of selecting appropriate methods is not a simple mechanical matter. It is a problem-solving response to highly complex situations. What teachers do at any moment must be appropriate to hundreds of factors in any situation. Teaching methods must fit the students (who are maddeningly diverse and individual), the subject, the environment, available equipment, school policies, rules and regulations, and the classroom. They must also fit the teacher's purposes, goals, knowledge, and experience, in addition to pupil needs, motivations, and goals. These are but a few of the more obvious factors that must be involved in a teacher's moment to moment choices. To fit all these conditions, the methods teachers use must be individual and unique. No wonder we cannot find specific behaviors or methods characteristic of good teaching or bad. The search for a common uniqueness is impossible by definition.

What makes a good teacher is a highly personal matter having to do with the teacher's personal system of perceptions or beliefs. To illustrate this point we can use the analogy of a computer that takes in vast quantities of information from outside, combines it with information already stored in its memory bank, and provides us, almost instantaneously, with answers for all the data. Teachers are like that. They take in great quantities of data moment by moment in the classroom. They combine this data with that from their own study and experience, and respond accordingly. In the computer, solutions to problems are determined by the program, usually a mathematical formula, placed in the machine by the operator. The "program" for teachers are the teacher's beliefs or perceptions.

People behave in terms of their beliefs. If I believe it is safe to cross the street, I do so. If I do not think it is safe, I wait. Everyone behaves in terms of his or her perceptions or beliefs, and teachers are no exception. It makes a great deal of difference how a teacher behaves toward a child, if the teacher believes the child is honestly trying or "goofing off." Teacher beliefs are crucial. They determine how teachers behave and how successful they are likely to be in carrying out their professional tasks.

Beliefs as Personal Theory

People's belief systems are the determiners of behavior. They provide the guidelines by which each of us selects appropriate behavior for the situations in which we find ourselves.[2] Our systems of beliefs represent our personal theories about how to deal with life. Everyone has a personal theory whether he or she has ever called it that or not. People behave in terms of their belief systems and other people quickly become aware of our characteristic perceptions or beliefs. They show in spite of us—so much so that people close to us can often predict our behavior with great accuracy. They say of us, "Well, he would!" or "Isn't that just like Helen to do that?"

The ways we behave reveal our beliefs to anyone who takes the trouble to try to read our behavior backwards. Here is an illustration. A few years ago I had to make a speech to what I believed would be a very hostile audience. I was fearful and unsure about whether I could make my case with any degree of success. I resolved simply to express my beliefs in the most direct fashion I could and leave the audience to react in whatever way they wished. To my surprise the speech went well. As I came down the steps from the rostrum, I was met by three acquaintances. The first one said, "Art, don't you just love it when you're up there and the spotlight's on you and there you are?" I looked at him in amazement. Here I had just survived a harrowing experience and he was talking about glorying in the limelight! Then I realized, that was why Paul liked to make speeches. The second acquaintance, holding out his fist said, "Wow! Art, you had them! Right there in your hand! You really had them!" For George the feeling of power was the important thing. The third acquaintance said, "Very adroit, Art, very adroit!" For Jack, what I had done was a neat trick, an intellectual caper! And for those of us who know him well, that was a precise expression of what Jack valued. Each of my friends was imputing to me his own values, revealing his own belief system for anyone to see—without being the slightest bit aware that he was doing so.

The Professional Need for Personal Theory

Theories are not right or wrong, only more or less valuable for confronting problems. For the scientist they are ways of organizing or examining events so that large amounts of information can be comprehended and organized for the scientist's purposes or to communicate with others in the scientific community.

Theories are equally important for the professional practitioner. They provide guidelines for practice. Indeed, possession of a comprehensive, congruent, and accurate frame of reference is a prime requisite in any truly professional activity. Responsible professional behavior demands that whatever the professional worker does must be defensible on some basis—research, theory, experience, expert opinion, or some other rational basis. In the medical profession physicians are not held responsible for the death of a patient; they *are* held responsible for being able to defend, in the eyes of their colleagues, that whatever was done had a reasonable presumption of being good for the patient. Similarly, it is not enough for a teacher who has accepted responsibility for helping students grow to simply "do what might work." Truly professional behavior demands more than that. It calls for belief systems as comprehensive, internally consistent, and accurate as teachers are capable of achieving.

CHARACTERISTICS OF EFFECTIVE PERSONAL THEORY

For some years I have been involved in a series of researches on effective practitioners in a number of helping professions, including teachers.[3] This experience leads me to the conclusion that the primary difference between good and poor teachers lies in their belief systems, the personal theories from which they make their choices. Personal theories of good teachers seem to have six important facets. They are: (1) comprehensive, (2) accurate, (3) internally congruent, (4) personally relevant, (5) appropriate to the tasks confronted, and (6) open to change.

1 Personal theory must be comprehensive. Personal theory can be very limited, applying only to minute aspects of life, or broad enough to provide guidelines for most of a person's activities. The belief systems of expert teachers are characteristically so all-embracing that their behaviors both in and out of the classroom seem governed by the same general principles and they are easily recognized as the same persons in whatever activities they engage. Less effective teachers, on the other hand, seem characterized by narrower personal theories restricted to specialized aspects of their activities. Often their behavior gives one the impression of "putting on an act," as though they were acting in ways they thought they should rather than proceeding from deeply held personal convictions. I once knew a famous child psychologist who, seven or eight years after marriage, finally had a new baby. I remember making the mistake of saying to him, "Congratulations, Ben, now you can talk like an expert!" He was not at all pleased. Instead, he drew himself up and haughtily replied, "I don't think that will make any difference." But it did!

Generally speaking, scientists seek the simplest possible explanations for ever more inclusive theoretical statements ($E = MC^2$, for example). This search for comprehensiveness can be clearly observed in the science of mathematics. In the course of human history, people needed to deal with countable things and developed a theory called arithmetic. Later, this frame of reference was no longer enough as people needed to solve problems involving unknown numbers—events that could not be directly observed or counted. So they developed algebra. Still later, even this was not enough and calculus was developed to deal with problems involving infinity. Each new theory does not deny what has gone before. Quite the contrary, broader frames of reference build upon and extend beyond less comprehensive ones.

The personal theories of good teachers include the broadest possible interpretations. The broader, more comprehensive one's personal theory, the more useful and trustworthy it becomes. Sometimes this comes about as a consequence of more experience but not necessarily. Simply living longer is no guarantee of a more comprehensive theory. Experience can be broadening. It can also be restricting. Even potentially enlightening experiences can fail to expand horizons if one is not open to and acceptant of events.

2   Theory must be accurate.   Personal theory must rest upon the most accurate bases available. It must be consistent with reality. Since people behave according to their beliefs, inaccurate ones result in inaccurate or ineffective behavior. What teachers do ought to be supportable on some reasonable basis. A theory out of touch with reality can hardly provide necessary signposts for effective action. Good theory must obviously be in line with the facts of life.

This is not as easy as it sounds for the question of what is real has baffled philosophers for generations and it is notorious that people have wide disagreements about even the simplest, most obvious "facts" of life. The teacher's personal theory can therefore never be unassailably correct. However, it can be tested by frequent confrontation with new or contradictory ideas. It can also be tested against the consequences of its use.

Expected or desirable outcomes provide a measure of proof that the theories from which they arose have some validity. Good theory must be able to stand the test of such examinations and teachers must stand ready to demonstrate that personal theories are based upon observations or concepts as accurate as can be obtained.

  3 Personal theory must be internally congruent. A personal theory with many contradictions or antagonistic concepts must, of necessity, result in inconsistent behavior on the part of the teacher with consequent incompatible messages delivered to students. "I believe that, but . . . " communications can be terribly confusing to students and colleagues resulting in the kind of equivocation and lack of assurance characteristic of inexperienced teachers. The success of persons in the helping professions is highly dependent on the stability and predictability of the helper and that, in turn, is largely dependent on an internally consistent personal theory in the helper.

  Many of the problems of beginning teachers are a consequence of inconsistent belief systems. Like building a house without a plan, beginning teachers lay on techniques with little or no awareness of the conflicting messages conveyed as a consequence of their own incongruent belief systems. Expert teachers, on the other hand, seem to have developed—either consciously or unconsciously—highly consistent systems of belief in the course of study and experience. The possession of such internally consistent belief systems provides the teacher with deep feelings of personal security. This, in turn, produces behavior so predictable and reasonable that other persons with whom the teacher interacts feel safe and comfortable. With consistent personal theories teachers have an aura of "being in command" of themselves and what they are about.

  4 Personal theory must be personally relevant. Whatever the nature of the teacher's personal theory, it must be more than mere knowledge to be espoused or declaimed in purely intellectual terms as the occasion demands.[4] It must be personally meaningful at so deep a level as to determine the teacher's behavior in all sorts of settings both in and out of professional life. We might represent the problem diagrammatically as a continuum from A to Z in which the Z end of the scale represents that knowledge or perception having little or no relationship to self.

Self   Not Self

At the opposite end of the continuum point A represents deeply meaningful perceptions, highly relevant to the person's self-organization. Information at point Z is perceived as having little relationship to self and therefore affects behavior only slightly, if at all. Perceptions close to point A have become so integral a part of the behaver's personal organization that they find expression in almost everything he or she does. Personal theory for the beginning practitioner is likely to rest somewhere near the Z end of the scale and can only be applied by thinking about it or "practicing" it. It represents a form of acting rather than a smooth expression of the person of the teacher. Most expert teachers have explored their personal meanings so often and so deeply that theory has become an in-depth part of their perceptual organizations or belief systems. This process is sometimes called *internalization,* but it is not so much a question of taking in an idea from outside as a matter of exploring and building, even creating, a personal frame of reference.

Ideas simply "known" but not regarded as truly significant for self are unlikely to be very helpful in providing clues to action. One can read all manner of theories, hear them expounded, and even agree that they are reasonable or right. One can understand ideas so well as to be able to pass a test about them or tell them to others, yet behave as though they did not exist if ideas have not been truly related to self. Effective theory requires commitment. Events perceived as "out there" are not likely to be used as bases for action except in half-hearted, tentative fashion. Events deeply identified with self, on the other hand, produce behavior which seems to other people to be authentic, appropriate and effortless.

5   Personal theory must be appropriate to the tasks confronted.   The beliefs that make up a personal theory of teaching must, of course, be appropriate for the tasks to which they are applied. In part, this requires the broad, comprehensive beliefs we previously mentioned in criterion #1. The more comprehensive the belief system, the more likely it is to contain the beliefs required for guidance in particular tasks. But even in a comprehensive system, inappropriate beliefs may be called upon for the selection of behavior. Beliefs in a personal theory do not exist in a jumbled mass. They are organized in terms of value and relevance and may result in vastly different choices. I have known teachers who valued self-determination so highly that children were encouraged to "express themselves" at the expense of learning to read. I have also known teachers so intent on teaching students to read that students were turned off from learning that vital skill for fear of humiliation and failure. It is possible to be so preoccupied with one goal that others are lost in the process so that "what one makes on the bananas one loses on the oranges." An adequate personal theory must be organized in some hierarchy of value and relevance if it is to provide the teacher with trust worthy guidelines for thinking and practice.

6 *Personal theory must always be open to change.* Truly effective theory must be adaptable. Times and circumstances change; goals, purposes, and people, including ourselves, also change. As a consequence, theories must constantly be kept current if they are to be maximally useful in providing direction for effective action. A theory frozen into rigidity will soon be out of touch with reality. Theories are not right or wrong, established once and forever. Theories are only ways of interpreting data. Personal theory must forever be open to new experience, ready to confront new events, to test, judge, reject, incorporate, or modify personal beliefs to accomodate new meanings. This does not mean that personal theory must drift willy-nilly with every new idea that appears on the horizon. Aspects of theory vary in degrees of significance. The most central or fundamental aspects of theory, if soundly based in the first place, may serve one well for a lifetime while more peripheral factors are adapting one way or another to changing times, circumstances, and ideas.

FACILITATING THE DEVELOPMENT
OF PERSONAL THEORY

The development of personal theory is a highly creative activity. It also takes time. For expert teachers it is a lifelong project, never reaching completion, but little by little achieving greater refinement and adequacy as teachers discover deeper and deeper meanings, more accurate perceptions, and greater internal congruence of concepts. Personal beliefs are not generally changed directly. They seldom develop by cataloging and analyzing one's beliefs or "deciding" to believe differently as an act of will. Rather, beliefs come into being, then change and develop as a consequence of acquiring meanings, usually in the course of solving problems or being involved in some life experience. Many kinds of experiences can make important contributions to personal beliefs. Among the most significant resources contributing to the development of my own personal theory are the following.

1 Reading, writing, and study.   There is a tremendous literature available in all aspects of professional education and in the basic sciences of psychology, sociology, anthropology, and biology which contribute to it. There are also a wide variety of study programs, lectures, workshops, demonstrations, and lab experiences available for the exploration of ideas and the expansion of teacher knowledge and skills. These may be found in teachers' colleges and under the auspices of special groups and professional organizations both in and out of education. All are important sources of information, ideas, and concepts for incorporation into a personal theory of teaching. As mere knowledge they are not likely to become dynamic aspects of personal theory, but personal meanings must begin somewhere and exposure to ideas is a necessary first step. Beyond that, each individual must somehow discover the personal meaning of new information or experience and fit them into the larger gestalt of personal theory. Schools and colleges have always accepted as their prime responsibility providing people with information. Until fairly recently they have not been so successful in finding ways to help people explore and discover personal meanings. But times are changing and all sorts of fascinating experiments are now going on both in and out of formal education to help students not only acquire information but discover its personal meanings as well.

An important device for helping me discover meaning is the discipline of writing. Writing forces me to explore my thinking. The process of finding ways to say things in such a manner that others can understand them clearly and precisely is at once a creative challenge for me, and a tremendous help in formulating my beliefs in more congruent and useful fashion.

2 *Interaction with significant others.* One of the most important ways most of us derive our personal belief systems is through interaction with the important persons in our lives. In the development of my personal belief system, for example, I have been deeply influenced by my wife, friends, colleagues at several universities, and acquaintance with several giants in education and psychology like Carl Rogers, Earl Kelley, Abe Maslow, Donald Snygg, and Sidney Pressey. Persons we love, admire, and respect provide enormous stimulation and direction to the development of one's personal theory—not only by what they have to say, but also by the examples they set in their own behavior.

3 *Personal and professional experience.* Perhaps the most powerful influences on personal beliefs are provided by one's experience. Most of us learn far more from events that happen to us or around us than from vicarious experiences provided by reading, lectures, audio-visual techniques, and the like. Teacher educators are keenly aware that student teachers learn far more from active classroom experience in the field than from all the lectures and demonstrations a teacher's college is able to provide. Through experience we have opportunities to test the accuracy of our assumptions. Even more important, however, is the value of experience in confronting learners with problems to be solved. Such confrontation forces us to examine beliefs and test them in action. It is a common saying among teachers, "I learned more than my students" and I find it is often true.

Of course it is possible to have much experience and still possess a weak, inaccurate, mixed-up system of beliefs. Some teachers build early defenses against learning from their professional experience. They spend much of their professional lives wearily plodding from day to day, mechanically meeting responsibilities in listless, cheerless fashion. People can learn good things from their experience. They can also become cynical, discouraged, and frustrated. What makes the difference is the attitude with which one's tasks are confronted. For those who are sensitive to the stimulation experiences provide, the potential for personal theory is great. Even a dismal failure can contribute to greater integration of personal theory. Indeed, if failure provides the shock required to reassess one's thinking, it may even prove of greater value than many successful experiences.

4   *Conversation and discussion.* For me one of the most valuable resources for theory building is interaction with others through almost any form of discussion. In such settings I have the opportunity to kick ideas around, to hear what others think and believe, to hear my own spontaneous expressions, and to have opportunites to assimilate the feedback from others as they agree or disagree, reject or embellish my beliefs. Such discussions may be formal or informal, in large groups or small, spontaneous or organized. So long as they provide opportunities for interaction and exploration of thinking, they serve a vital function in ordering the development of personal theory. Of course not all discussions are of equal significance for theory development. Much depends on the level of talk and the nature of topics under exploration. I am not much stimulated by rehashing things I have long since settled or dealing with events on so superficial a level as to represent little more than a bull session or gossip.

An important contribution of modern interest in awareness, sensitivity, and encounter groups is the opportunity such group techniques have provided us for stimulating effective group interaction and in-depth exploration of attitudes, beliefs, feelings, and values about one's self, others, and the world. Opportunities for participating in such groups under skilled and responsible leadership are more and more widely available and can contribute much to exploration and discovery of new personal meaning.

5 *Experimentation and innovation.* Another important way in which personal theory can be explored is through experiment and innovation. These provide opportunities to test the validity of personal theories in action. Even more, developing an experiment or innovation inevitably confronts the experimenter with new problems, and the resolution of such problems in turn contributes much to the growth and refinement of personal theory. Daring to try, daring to confront the unknown, is the first requirement for creative experience. The status quo is comfortable and secure, but offers little in the way of stimulation for change and development. Unfortunately, many aspects of educational organization, administration, and practice militate against experimenting and innovating. Fear of making mistakes also immobilizes teachers and administrators to such an extent that experimentation and innovation may be discouraged or forbidden. Every teacher, however, has innumerable opportunities for trying new things in his or her own classroom even if administrators and supervisory personnel discourage innovation in the broader aspects of curriculum and organization. By taking advantage of those possibilities directly within one's own control, the value of experimentation and innovation for personal exploration can be realized no matter what the attitudes of people elsewhere.

6 *Confrontation.* An important source of stimulation for personal theory developent lies in confrontation with people and problems wherever they may be found. Some of our most important learnings take place as a consequence of mistakes or times when we are brought face to face with a major or minor crisis and so are forced in dramatic fashion to examine our fundamental beliefs. Learning comes about as a consequence of the need to solve problems, and confrontation presents us with problems in ways that do not permit avoidance or escape. They demand attention. Sometimes they are also painful. Nevertheless,

they contribute to sorting out thinking, opening new avenues, and beginning the process of exploration and discovery.

Incongruities in personal theory can often be brought to light by confronting "ultimate questions." This is a process of pushing beliefs to extremes as a way of determining just how strongly they are held. Some typical examples might be confronting questions like:

How firmly do I believe in the confidentiality of my relationship with students? How will I behave if a colleague asks me what happened in an interview? If the principal makes such a request? If such information is demanded by the student's parents? If I am ordered by a court of law to divulge information?

How much do I believe in the basic democratic tenet that "when people are free they can find their own best ways"? To let students participate in student government? To participate in classroom planning? To do their own policing of halls and cafeteria? To drop out of school?

In the answers a teacher finds to such questions, he or she may also find a measure of the depth and congruence of various aspects of personal theory.

7   *Counseling and psychotherapy.* Another valuable resource for exploring personal theory is participation as a client in counseling and psychotherapy. Such resources are particularly valuable for the exploration of those very personal aspects of one's beliefs about self and others which often cannot be explored in the ordinary settings of daily life. Counseling and psychotherapy create a kind of special relationship in which a person may be temporarily protected from the pressures of daily existence and helped to explore deeply personal feelings, attitudes, and beliefs with the assistance of someone especially trained for that purpose.

One does not have to be crazy or sick to take advantage of such services. A good counselor or therapist can be immensely helpful in facilitating the process of setting one's thinking in better order, no matter what the topic. I have frequently used the services of professional counselors in my own lifetime. Sometimes I have sought such help because I was trying to find my way through deeply personal "psychological" problems of one sort or another. At other times I have sought the experience of counseling simply in order to clarify my thinking, explore ideas, or seek for solutions to quite academic questions that did not involve any sense of crisis whatever. I have never regretted these experiences. Quite the contrary. Looking back over my life from my present vantage point I can see how some stand out as times when I made critical decisions or changes in life direction. Others were times of consolidating gains and exploring the meaning of new events and circumstances. All made significant contributions to a fuller, richer, personal theory.

THE INGREDIENTS OF EFFECTIVE PERSONAL THEORY

To this point I have listed criteria for determining what good personal theory is like. I have also suggested resources from which the beliefs that make up a theory can be drawn. What makes a personal theory functional, however, is the nature of the beliefs it contains. It is the content of beliefs, what they are about, that determines professional behavior. In the remainder of this book I intend to set down the major beliefs in my personal theory of teaching in the hope that such sharing may be useful to others.

Of course, the beliefs in anyone's personal theory cover a vast field of events. Some beliefs will be very general applying to almost everything a teacher does. Beliefs about how people learn, for instance, affect teacher behavior at all levels, from nursery school to college or anywhere between. On the other hand, beliefs about an aspect of the particular subject one teaches or one's beliefs about the performance of a particular student are so specific as to be of little value for anyone else. I have therefore restricted this outline of my personal theory to those aspects of broadest possible relevance.

For nearly twenty years I have been deeply involved in a series of researches designed to explore the belief systems of good and poor workers in a number of helping professions, including teaching.[5] These studies suggest that the crucial beliefs of good teachers fall generally in six major areas:

1 The nature and possibilities of the human organism. What people are like and what can be expected of them.
2 The psychology of persons. The how and why of human behavior.
3 Beliefs about learning. How people grow and change.
4 Goals and purposes. What persons and societies are striving for.
5 Appropriate methods. How people select the techniques they use to achieve their purposes.
6 About self. What teachers believe about themselves and how this determines their behavior.

The areas suggested by these researches seem so vital that I have used them to present my personal theory in the pages that follow. I also added a category not included in any research I know of to date—the teacher's beliefs about the future. A major purpose of education is the preparation of youth for the future. Whatever we believe about those matters must therefore deeply affect educational thinking and practice.

CHAPTER 2

Origins and Possibilities

Some people believe the human organism is essentially good; others believe our basic nature is fundamentally evil. Still others see the human organism as a kind of battleground in which the forces of good and evil are locked in perpetual struggle. Not me. I do not believe the organism comes into the world either good or evil. The labels "good" or "evil" are descriptive judgments our culture applies to the ways people behave. At birth we just *are*. In later life what we do or become may be described as good or evil, but we were not born so.

THE BASIC DRIVE TOWARD HEALTH

This is not to say that the human organism is passive or without direction. Quite the contrary. From the moment of conception we begin an insatiable search for wholeness or health which never ceases until death has occurred in the last of our cells. This insatiable drive toward health is characteristic of protoplasm itself—the stuff of life. Even the lowliest single-celled animals oozing about in a drop of water move *away* from danger or injury and *toward* food or better conditions for growth. If they didn't they would not long survive. The drive toward health is a built-in quality of every living cell, including the millions that make up a complex human being.[1]

Looking about us we can find examples of this basic drive in all living things. Injured trees grow new bark, grasses run over by a car soon return to an upright condition, wounds heal, plants grow toward the light, a cat that has lost a leg learns to get about on three. Everywhere living things are seeking to maintain life—Not just any life, but the best they can.

The practice of medicine is predicated on the organism's drive toward health. The doctor doesn't cure us; our bodies do that automatically if they can. What doctors do is help create conditions that will make it possible for the basic drive toward fulfillment to operate with greatest possible freedom. They may do this by removing a diseased organ, by destroying or counteracting the influence of some germ that has invaded the body, or by building up the body resources through rest, exercise, or diet. But in the final analysis, the body gets well of itself propelled by its own basic need.

Other professions are equally dependent upon the organism's striving for fulfillment. Counselors, for example, help clients explore themselves and the world in which they live in the search for new and better solutions to personal problems. The client's drive for health motivates the search and new, more satisfying ways of behaving come into being as clients discover new ways of perceiving self and the world. Social workers help clients in similar fashion. Teachers, too, must learn to work *with* the need for fulfillment. They cannot *make* people learn. They can only create conditions that will help students learn for themselves. If teachers succeed at that, the student's own need for growth can be counted upon to provide the motives for learning.

For human beings the search for health and fulfillment has many more possibilities than in simpler animals. In low-order animals the basic drive is expressed exclusively in physical terms. The amoeba can only respond to that which touches its surface and it responds in ways to maintain its physical self. People are much more complex. For one thing, our highly developed sense organs make it possible to deal with events that haven't happened yet. Because we have eyes and ears, we can respond to matters at a distance that have not touched us physically. This greatly expanded awareness means we can interact with a fantastically rich world of possibilities. We can even deal with the future.

The Self We Seek to Fulfill

There is an even more important way in which the human drive to health is different from lower orders of life. People do not seek only to maintain or fulfill the physical self. We seek fulfillment of a much larger self—the self of which we are aware—the phenomenal self or self-concept. We seek fulfillment of ourselves as "persons." The self we seek to maintain is the person we describe as "I" or "me"—Hiroshi Matsumo, Susan Smith, John Brown, or Carlotta Martinez. The phenomenal self or self-concept is our experienced self, the person one believes he or she is.

This phenomenal self, self-concept, or self as person is far more complex than the physical self. It has thousands of definitions with varying degrees of centrality or importance to the owner. A particular person, for example, might see himself as Jonathan Maxwell, male, five feet ten inches, with brown hair, brown eyes, and growing bald. He might also see himself as a husband, father of three children, teacher, fair tennis player, bad skier, and good businessman. His self-definitions might also include such ideas as "I like to keep a good-looking lawn," "People don't like me much," or "I wish I was a better father to my kids." These are but a few of the beliefs that comprise Jonathan Maxwell as seen from his own point of view.

The phenomenal self is so important for most of us that we may even place our physical selves in jeopardy to achieve the maintenance or enhancement of the self we experience. We may drive too fast because it feels good even though we know it is dangerous. We may smoke, drink too much, eat very badly, or engage in dangerous sports because the self we wish to fulfill is not our physical self but our personal one. People starve themselves or go to prison for principles that seem more important than their physical selves. Even suicide is motivated by the need to maintain or enhance the phenomenal self. Persons may willingly die, for example, for the sake of a cause they are identified with or to avoid even greater misery they can see ahead. The self we experience is far more important to us than the body in which it travels.

Because we humans are aware of the future we seek much more than mere survival. The maintenance we seek extends beyond the present to encompass future needs. We seek the maintenance of self not just for today, but for the forseeable future as well. This calls for building a self capable of more than holding the line. We seek to make ourselves stronger, more attractive, richer, or better in whatever ways seem most personally promising or fulfilling. Our basic need requires enhancement or fulfillment—making the self as adequate as possible.

The human organism is certainly not evil; neither is it necessarily good. It is also not a battleground of conflicting natures. Quite the contrary; it is always motivated toward a single basic goal—health and fulfillment. Perhaps the best we can say of such a drive is that it seems more positive than negative.

The Human Organism Is Trustworthy

The existence of a fundamental drive toward health and fulfillment rooted in protoplasm itself means the human organism is essentially trustworthy. It can, it will, it must move toward health and fulfillment if the way seems open to do so. At first glance such a statement about our fundamental nature may seem exaggerated or naive. I thought so once myself. It took a lot of study, a lot of involvement with clients in psychotherapy and students in classes and laboratories, and much personal experience in living before I came to feel the full impact of such an understanding for my whole way of life.

The Big "If"

Simply looking about, anyone can observe innumerable instances in which people seem to be behaving in pretty untrustworthy fashion. They harm themselves. They harm other people in straight out hostility or through subtle and crafty devices. I am not so naive as to trust "just anyone" in spite of my firm belief that people can, will, and must move toward health if the way seems open to do so. The catch in that statement is the big "if"—if the way seems open to them. The basic drive in each of us is insatiable. How and where it is expressed in a person's behavior, however, is dependent on what that person believes is possible and desirable.

I may believe my son should go to college; however, unless he believes it desirable and possible, I'd better not set my heart on it. People behave according to how things seem to them, not how they look to outsiders. People can be trusted to move toward health in ways that seem open and desirable from *their points of view*. What seems like a road to health and fulfillment is a purely personal matter and each of us seeks fulfillment in ways that seem personally appropriate. Our choices may seem misguided to outsiders, but our behavior always seems reasonable to us at the moment of acting.

People do, indeed, behave in stupid, maladaptive, and destructive ways. This is not because the need for fulfillment has gone berserk. They still seek health and fulfillment—but as they see it! Take the case of a delinquent, Tim Simpson: Growing up with repeated experiences of failure at home, in school, and in the community, Tim came to feel inadequate as a person. In time, as he found himself repeatedly frustrated in interactions with the world about him he also came to feel, "Nobody likes me. Nobody wants me. Nobody cares about me." With continued negative experience, some of which may be brought about by people's reactions to Tim's own behavior, he may finally arrive at the logical conclusion, "Well I don't like nobody neither!" At this point what he does to fulfill himself by getting the best of others may be unacceptable, even dangerous to people around him. They, in turn, behave toward Tim with further rejection which only serves to prove to Tim what he already believes. This self-perpetuating spiral can end in tragedy for Tim as it has for countless delinquents before him. Tim's drive to fulfillment is still there and still operating. His unfortunate ways of seeing himself and the world, however, provide inadequate bases from which to make his choices.

Persons can, will, must move toward health *if* the way seems open for them to do so. Dealing with this *if* is what the helping professions are all about. The task of the counselor, psychotherapist, social worker, or teacher is to create conditions that set the drive to fulfillment free to operate with less distortion. They do this by helping patients, clients, and students perceive themselves and their worlds in more adequate ways. The counselor, for example, may help a puzzled mother explore herself, her feelings, her goals, and the situations she finds herself in. As she sees these matters more clearly, she may then be helped to perceive more satisfying ways of relating with her children. The psychotherapist operates in a similar manner to help a husband and wife arrive at new ways of seeing themselves and their relationships so that their fundamental drives toward fulfillment will be more likely to be achieved. The task of the social worker is similarly concentrated on helping clients perceive new and better ways of living effectively in the community. Education, too, is engaged in this process. Stupid people are not very free. Helping students achieve greater awareness of themselves and the world they are living in is to expand their horizons and so provide greater freedom for the fundamental drive for fulfillment to operate.

HUMAN POSSIBILITIES

A second belief about our fundamental nature which pervades every aspect of my philosophy and practice has to do with what is possible for persons. Some people are deeply impressed with the ways in which we are limited—physically, intellectually, emotionally. They believe we come into the world with an established set of capacities, and thereafter there is little we can do to exceed them. Until fairly recent years many psychologists thought so, too. I used to share that idea. No more. I am now convinced we have been selling people short for generations. Today I am far more impressed with human possibilities or potentialities. In fact, I have come to believe the potentialities of persons for effective behavior are almost limitless.

It is true we are all limited by the physical bodies in which we live. We cannot fly like birds, swim like seals, or run with the speed and grace of an antelope. Many of us have also experienced changes in body capacity with advancing age, disease, or injury. Most of us are keenly aware of our physical limits and we are accustomed to thinking about human possibilities in those terms. We assume that all our potentialities are limited in the same manner as our bodies. For many years psychologists believed this, too. They described the capacities of human beings to behave intelligently and wisely primarily as a hereditary matter. They believed that people were born with strict limits on intelligence beyond which they could not hope to rise and constructed tests to measure this innate capacity. These ideas were in line with what people in general already believed and the psychologists' opinion gave it the apparent endorsement of "science." There are still many places where one can find intelligence scores treated with the same acceptance as a doctor's prescription. More recently we have come to understand that this is much too narrow a view of human capacities.

Our Physical Potentials

Modern science has helped us realize that the human organism is extraordinarily tough and resilient with capacities far greater than we formerly believed. Indeed, the most fascinating thing about our physical selves is not our limitations but our fantastic possibilities.[2] Few of us use more than a small portion of what is possible. In recent years, for example, we have seen great extensions of our physical limits as more and more people have gotten involved in health related activities like diet, exercise, running, relaxation, and the like. Almost everyone can relate instances of extraordinary strength or endurance manifest by persons we know about. Just as the engineer constructing a dam builds into the structure a capacity to withstand stresses and strains far beyond anything the dam will ever be expected to support, just so, the human organism is overbuilt. Few of us ever use more than a small percentage of our total possibilities. In the course of evolution it had to be so. If the human organism had not been able to rise to the occasion and deal with emergencies, the human race would have died out long ago.

Behavioral Capacities

The capacities of human beings also extend far beyond their physical bodies. For most of us, success in life and happiness in living are far more dependent on behavioral, intellectual, or emotional aspects of being. How we act as persons, how well we do our jobs, relate to other people, manipulate tools, machinery, or equipment generally requires little more than minimum physical prowess. What we think and believe or what we feel, like, dislike, love, hate, and aspire to are even less dependent upon physical condition. With respect to such matters, so far as we can tell, human possibilities are practically limitless.

To understand the almost limitless character of human behavioral potential I find it helpful to draw an analogy with the concept in physics of "critical mass." In building an atomic reaction, events occur in smooth predictable fashion as radioactive material is increased to the critical mass. Then an explosion takes place, all conditions change and a vast release of power occurs. In similar fashion, once a human being is possessed of the necessary physical equipment for perceiving and behaving, constraints of the body are no longer the crucial determining factors and the possibilities for perceiving and behaving are vast beyond measure.

Our physical bodies provide the vehicle for thinking, feeling, seeing, hearing, and comprehending. Once we possess the machinery to make those functions possible, what is seen, heard, or understood is primarily determined by nonphysical conditions. Take the matter of seeing. Once a person has eyes capable of seeing in reasonably adequate fashion, after that, what he or she has seen, is seeing now, or is likely to see in the future cannot be understood by a study of the eyes alone. Given the physical equipment to make experience possible, what is thereafter experienced is practically limitless. Behavior is learned and possibilities for learning have almost no end. This is a concept of fantastic importance to educators. If thinking, feeling, knowing, and understanding are learned capacities, they can be taught and teachers can help to produce them. These are also determiners of behavior that govern whether or not we behave in intelligent fashion. So, intelligence itself can be created.[3] That exciting discovery provides new hope for teaching and imposes a vast new challenge for our educational system.

Of course, there are limits to how people behave, think, feel, and believe. Such limits are not inborn, however; they are learned in the course of growing up. That does not mean they are any less significant. Learned restraints can be just as insidious and handicapping as innate physical limits. But the fact that they are acquired, that they are not "in the nature of the beast," is, itself, a matter of tremendous importance. Limits that are learned can be unlearned—innate limits we are stuck with forever.

THE HUMAN ORGANISM IS UNIQUE AND PRECIOUS

A third basic characteristic of the human organism important to my personal theory of teaching is uniqueness. Scientists tell us that at the moment of conception the determining genes carried by the sperm and egg are so complex that the resulting fertilized ovum, embryo, fetus, child is absolutely unique. In all of history there has never been another like it and in all of time ahead there will never be another. Each human being is one of its kind for all times.[4]

Even if a child's genetic history did not make him or her unique, experience after conception would. We are products of our experience and no two people can ever have the same experience. Even children born in the same family do not have the same experience. Just the fact of being the first child, middle child, youngest child, or only child means different kinds of experience for each of us. Even in the case of identical twins, the environment of Twin A is Twin B and the environment of Twin B is Twin A.

The uniqueness of persons is perhaps the most important fact about them. We are born unique and become ever more diverse the longer we live. This is the normal, natural flow of life. It is also a reason for the immense value of individuals. Each human being is a unique creation and each is capable of contributing something special to the world. Each of us has something or knows something that no one else can have or know in just that way. We are inherently valuable.

A complex society like ours is totally dependent on the uniqueness of its citizens. Ours is probably the most complex interdependent society the world has ever known. We are thoroughly dependent on each other. Such a society requires a smooth integration of millions of individuals willing and able to contribute their special talents, knowledge and skills to the welfare of the whole, while at the same time fulfilling their personal needs as individuals. To achieve personal fulfillment can only be accomplished for most of us by contributing to the fulfillment of others as well. The progress of society is, therefore, dependent on each individual willingly fitting his or her uniqueness into a smooth-running whole while simultaneously achieving personal significance. Whatever impedes or destroys this progress is a dreadful loss to all of us.

Uniqueness of the human organism means that persons are rare and precious. A person lost is a loss forever. Earl Kelley believed very deeply in the uniqueness of human beings and frequently wrote about the significance of student individuality for education.[5] He once wrote me, "Art, you must take good care of yourself for there is only one of you and we can't afford to lose you." To Kelley each person was precious just for being. The founders of our democratic society believed that too. So do I.

PRACTICAL IMPLICATIONS

The view of human nature I have been outlining in this chapter should not be described as a hopeful one. That word implies a fundamental lack of confidence in the basic character of human beings. I do not just hope human beings are unique, have enormous potential, and are basically motivated toward health. The view I have been outlining is a confident, positive view firmly grounded in biological research and the observations and conclusions of many more persons than me. I have absolute confidence in its accuracy and I find it expressed in all my contacts with students.

I am convinced that a great many problems of education down the years have been the consequence of inaccurate concepts of the nature of the organism—children or youth. Young people new to the profession do not choose their concepts of human nature and capacity. They acquire them by osmosis from the people who surround them in the process of growing up. Later, they find them confirmed in the course of their professional training and buttressed by the attitudes of teachers around them on the job. So, faulty beliefs continue from generation to generation determining choices and actions that often defeat the very goals of education. That's bad enough, in itself. Too often, the mischief extends to children and youth who are the unwitting victims of the process.

I do not find my students either angels or devils. They are all unique individuals with built-in positive motivation. The particular expressions of their fundamental need are not always the same as mine, but always toward health and fulfillment as they perceive it. Students have tremendous potential. They don't always use their capacities in ways I might wish, but the possibilities are there waiting to be released if the student and I can find the keys to set it free.

Student Need and Teaching

The fundamental need of the organism for maintenance and enhancement or self-fulfillment has enormous implications for teaching. What seems to a person to affect his or her basic need in some vital way must be attended to. Few of us are able to set aside our search for need satisfaction for more than very short intervals. Less pressing expressions like getting a drink of water, going to a movie, reading the paper, or doing one's homework can easily be postponed or diverted. Primary expressions like intense hunger, fear, threats to self-esteem, deprivations of love, belonging, and the like are, for most people, so important that satisfaction can be set aside only for very brief periods if at all.

This means for me that effective learning must begin with awareness of student needs. Personal needs are compelling and immediate. Motivating people to learn something because "they might need it someday" may seem basic to adults, but student needs exist in the here and now. Important student problems, just as for adults, cannot be easily set aside for remote or less pressing ones. Yet much of education is focused upon preparing students for problems they will have sometime in the nebulous future.

This discrepancy between student perception of what is currently or personally important and society's beliefs about what "ought" to be important creates continuous problems for education. One way schools have tried to solve the dilemma is by creating artificial needs for learning like grades, honors, token rewards, or teacher approval. Since real, personal needs take precedence over artificial ones, such devices are notoriously disappointing except for those few students whose basic needs are already fairly well met or those who can be seduced into believing that artificial satisfactions are truly worth while.

Welch and Usher point out that school "refusal to meet students needs has always been backed by some mention of standards of academic, program or institutional excellence; as if meeting students' concerns and excellence were discrete categories. Yet, we are coming to realize that personal meaning is the door through which facts pass before behavior is changed. Before education can make a difference in the lives of students it must meet their needs. How can a teacher know if the facts in which she is dealing are relevant to every individual in class? She cannot and that is the point. The only way we can approach relevance is by allowing greater choice in our classroom."[6]

Since students' primary needs are so demanding, I see no alternative for effective teaching than to assure that somewhere in the processes of education student needs are recognized and fulfilled—at least as far as the school and its teachers are able to do so. If personal needs preoccupy my students so that they are not able to perceive what I wish for them, then I must begin by helping students achieve some measure of fulfillment of their personal needs. I may not be able to do that as well as I might wish, but I have to make the effort. Sometimes this may be accomplished by events outside the school setting or through agencies in the community, sometimes through services within the school organization, and sometimes I can affect those forces or help students come in touch with them. I can also contribute in some measure to student's personal need satisfaction in my classroom if I am sufficiently sensitive to students and care enough about helping them to learn. Better yet, if I can help students perceive that the subject I teach, the way I teach it, and their interactions with me are personally need-fulfilling, then we both gain from the process. The student's own need provides motivation to learn and I can feel more successful as a teacher. Working *with* student needs instead of against them is far more likely to produce effective learning.

That good teaching begins with helping students fulfill basic needs does not mean good teaching stops there. I have known schools established especially for deeply deprived, so-called problem children, which concentrate so much upon filling the student's personal needs through eliminating coercion and surrounding students with a loving, caring faculty as to practically eliminate any semblance of traditional curricula. There is a place for schools like that and Lord knows there are children enough who need them. Most public schools, however, must move beyond such rehabilitative measures. It is not enough to simply satisfy student needs. The genius of good teaching lies in helping students discover needs they never knew they had. The most effective schools and teachers do more than satisfy existing student needs; they turn students on. They help students perceive ever broader horizons and greater depths of experience.

Creating Expectations

A number of researches on the differences between good and poor teachers have found that good teachers perceive students as essentially able, while poor ones have grave doubts about student ability. Good teachers also perceive students as trustworthy, while poor teachers regard them as untrustworthy.[7] It makes a great deal of difference what teachers believe about student abilities and motives. Teachers who do not believe students are able, for example, dare not let them. To let students make decisions, if you do not believe they can be trusted, is irresponsible.

Teachers who see students as unable are defeated before they begin and their teaching is likely to devolve into spiritless plodding toward hopeless goals or attacks upon students for their perversity, apathy, or stupidity. I feel very sorry for such teachers. Life must be a pretty dreary grind for them. My belief in the capacities of students and the organism's basic need for health and fulfillment spares me such discouragement. Instead, I can approach my profession with confidence, hope and the assurance that I can be a significant and positive factor in student growth.

There is a good deal of research to show that people tend to respond in terms of the expectancies of those who surround them. A teacher once told me that at the beginning of the school year she looked up the intelligence test records of the children in her class. Near the end of the year another teacher said to her, "What on earth have you done with Jimmy? I never would have believed it! Last year he was one of the dumbest kids in my class." My teacher friend was astonished for she counted Jimmy among her better students. Although he started the year slowly, he was now in the upper fourth of her class. With embarrassment, she told me, "When I heard that about Jimmy, I went back to look at his records and you know what I found? At the beginning of the year I put down his locker number instead of his IQ! His locker number was 123; his IQ was 94. Wasn't that dumb?" It was not dumb for Jimmy. He lived up to what his teacher expected of him. What teachers believe determines the methods they use; the methods they use, in turn, convey messages to students about teacher attitudes and expectations.

Trusting Students

A great deal of what we do in schools begins from the premise that kids can't be trusted—and we pay the penalty for it. In his book *Fit for Freedom,* Professor Phil Constans says, "We don't trust kids. Or, to put it another way, because there *are some* kids that we can't trust, we have a strong tendency to treat all our students as though they can't be trusted. Take a hard look at a set of school rules and you'll see what I mean. Almost without exception we establish our rules in terms of the worst actions of the worst element in our population. When we do this, we put ourselves in the position of treating the overwhelming majority of our students, whom I believe can be trusted, as though they were untrustworthy. Having arrived at this position, it is an easy step to viewing the student body as a group committed to getting away with things, beating the system, evading the ever increasing list of rules, and subverting the best efforts of the faculty. Once we start thinking this way, the role of the faculty automatically becomes one of checking, searching, watching and catching. Ergo, 'the student as enemy.' If you think this doesn't happen sit and listen to the talk in almost any teachers' lounge."[8]

Seeing the human organism as one of immense potentialities, infinite uniqueness and forever motivated to move toward fulfillment deeply affects my thinking and practice. For one thing, I can operate from the assumption that both the student and I want the same thing—the student's health and fulfillment. That puts us on the same side of the fence. We may differ in our conceptions of how best to reach that objective, but, at least we start with a common goal. Many teachers unfortunately see students as "the enemy," people who the teacher is expected to educate in spite of themselves. Since people behave according to their expectations, such assumptions about student motives are asking for trouble. Communicating with the enemy is not likely to be very effective. What is more, persons we regard as enemies are generally willing to oblige by acting so.

For many years I have used a contract method of grading which places a great deal of responsibility on the student for developing and carrying out the terms of his contract. My experience has been that the overwhelming majority of students work harder, produce more, and learn more from such treatment. Such a system requires that the instructor put a great deal of trust in the students. Occasionally students do not live up to my expectations, but that is because past experiences have taught them to be devious or current pressures are so great they succumb to the temptation to be dishonest. Most students live up to the trust I place in them. Even if they did not I would continue my practice. People can't learn about trust unless someone trusts them. A student once said to me, "Art, do you know that some students take advantage of your contract grading system?" When I told him I was aware that now and then someone did that, he said, "I guess it doesn't bother you, does it?"

He thought a moment and continued, "Well, that figures, the old system took advantage of the student!" Trusting folks requires running some risks. Withholding trust for fear of those risks negates the very experience by which trust in people is learned.

A More Relaxed Approach to Teaching

Because I believe in the fundamental trustworthiness of the human organism, I can be more relaxed in carrying out my professional responsibilities. Understanding that students can, will, must move toward health if the way seems open to them to do so helps me to be more tolerant and accepting of students. After all, if every human being is constantly seeking to move toward health, then who shall we blame for what? Instead of spending time in recriminations or bemoaning the nature of students, things I cannot change, I can get about the business of focusing on matters I can do something about. I can zero in on creating conditions that will make it possible for students to move toward fulfillment more effectively. As I succeed in that, both students and I can experience the fruits of success.

Believing in the uniqueness of every individual, I can accept and appreciate difference instead of fighting it. I do not get caught in the problems and frustrations of expecting everyone to be at the same place at the same time. For me individual instruction is more than a high sounding educational objective. It is a necessity required by the fundamental uniqueness of the human organism. Understanding uniqueness is also helpful in dealing with such pressing problems as desegregation, ethnic differences, and the demands of youth for greater respect and autonomy.

Knowing that human beings can, will, must move toward health if the way seems open for them to do so means I do not have to *make* students learn or behave. Trying to *make* people do things requires an enormous amount of energy and seldom achieves very permanent results. The old saying "A man convinced against his will is of the same opinion still" is more often true than not. My teaching goes much better when I concentrate my attention on creating the best conditions I know how to arrange for student growth and development. If I can do that well I can rest assured that students will make significant progress. This understanding takes a great load from my shoulders. In place of guilt over what I cannot control, I am freed to concentrate on things I can control—my own behavior and professional skills.

Some Effects on Student-Teacher Relationships

Perhaps the most satisfying aspect of my beliefs about the nature of the organism occurs in respect to teacher-student relationships. Real trust in the organism, awareness of student uniqueness, and belief in the almost unlimited scope of human capacities is inevitably expressed in the attitudes and behavior of teachers. Students, in turn, "get the message" from such experiences and respond accordingly. It is hard to hate or dislike someone who believes in you and demonstrates faith in your uniqueness, capacity, and worth. As a consequence, the interactions I have with students are more likely to be friendly and cooperative relationships from which both they and I derive important satisfactions. Research on teacher-pupil relationships has repeatedly demonstrated that students tend to live up to the expectations of teachers. Teachers who exude positive beliefs about students are thus likely to find their beliefs confirmed in greater student interest, involvement, commitment, expenditures of effort, higher achievement, and fewer discipline problems. Under such conditions, everyone wins.

Believing in the uniqueness, potentialities, and positive motivation of the human organism means teachers can have confidence that people can, will, must move toward fulfillment if the way is open to them.[9] That belief, in turn, provides a broad base of security for me. Tackling a job is uphill work if one feels goals cannot be reached or the people one must work with are hostile and perverse. Believing in the positive character of the human organism I can be free of such shackles to get on with the more important task of dealing with the big *if*—creating conditions that will free the student's need, potential, and uniqueness to seek its fullest possible expression. How well that objective is accomplished will be dependent upon beliefs about other matters, especially about the causes of behavior and how it changes. That is the topic of Chapter 3.

CHAPTER 3

About Behavior and Its Causes

In order to carry out their professional responsibilities teachers need a working theory of how and why people behave or misbehave. There are a number of psychological theories available on which one may draw for ideas to be incorporated into a personal theory of teaching. Some of these are limited in scope, some are all inclusive, some are old, and some are new. Some are so complex and technical as to be useful only for professional psychologists in talking to each other. Others are too narrowly specialized to provide much guidance for dealing with classroom problems. For the most part my personal theory of teaching is drawn from two general approaches for understanding people and their behavior. One of these is behaviorism, whose concepts I find useful when my primary goals are the management of student behavior or the teaching of specific skills or ways of behaving. The other is perceptual psychology, which I turn to when my purposes are defined in broader, holistic terms or when I am more concerned with the teaching of processes than ends.

BEHAVIORISTIC PSYCHOLOGY

One way to understand human beings is to look at them externally, to examine their behavior and interactions with the world from the point of view of a disinterested observer. This is the approach characteristic of most psychologies in the United States for the past fifty years. It is called behavioristic, or S-R psychology because it seeks understanding of behavior in terms of stimulus and response. Typical examples are: Drivers stop for red lights and go for green ones; students work for rewards and seek to avoid punishment. Behaviorism treats behavior as a product of the stimuli or forces exerted upon a person now or in the past. Motivation, in such systems, is primarily a matter of the manipulation of external events in such manner that the subject behaves in the fashion desired by those applying the forces. This general point of view about persons has had many proponents over the past fifty years. It has produced a vast literature of research and theory contributing enormously to our understanding of the nature of behavior and the forces impinging upon it. A major offshoot in more recent years has been behavior modification, a school of thought which sees behavior as a function of its consequents. Many psychologists operating in this frame of reference have been deeply interested in problems of teaching and have made important contributions to educational practice.[1]

Behavioristic psychology can be very useful in helping us understand, guide, or control persons in situations where particular behavior outcomes are clearly defined and where the forces affecting a person's behavior are within the teacher's control. Sample uses might be teaching a child basic skills, especially when these can be broken down into fairly simple elements. Behavioral approaches can also be used for the management of student behavior toward specific goals when these can be precisely defined. Teachers at any level will often be seeking objectives for which behavioral psychology can provide important guidance and the potential contributions of behavioral thinking ought to be part of a mature teacher's personal theory of teaching.

While behavioral thinking will often be useful, it is not enough, by itself, to provide the comprehensive personal theory required for effective teaching. Education for the world we live in requires much more of students than acquisition of precisely defined skills or behaviors. It must contribute as well to their internal growth and prepare them to live in a future that cannot be accurately predicted. Such a goal as intelligent behavior, for example, cannot be defined in terms of particular outcomes. It requires that persons be able to confront unforeseen problems and find appropriate solutions for them. If intelligent behavior could be precisely predicted, it would not be intelligent, it would be mechanical. Similarly, objectives like worthy home membership, mental health, job satisfaction, or responsible participation in society are primarily dependent upon generalized attitudes, feelings, emotions, or values rather than precisely defined behaviors. To deal with such objectives a broader, more comprehensive psychology is needed.

A PERCEPTUAL VIEW OF HUMAN BEHAVIOR

Increasing numbers of American psychologists have come to regard the behavioral frame of reference as too limited a view of persons and behavior. Many workers in such helping professions as counseling, psychotherapy, group work, teaching, pastoral care, and human relations activities have found behavioral concepts inadequate for dealing with experiential, personal aspects of human growth and existence. As a consequence some psychologists have sought more adequate ways to explore such personal matters as human awareness, experience, the place of perceptions, values, beliefs, feelings, emotion, choice, will, self-actualization, self-transcendence, expanding consciousness, being, and becoming. This expanded view of psychology is often called "the third force" or "the humanist movement."[2] It has produced a number of new psychologies under such titles as humanistic, experiential, personal, self, phenomenological, perceptual, and existential psychology. All are concerned with the personal, experiential aspects of persons—the things that make us human.

I have been deeply involved with the humanist movement in psychology all my professional life. In collaboration with Donald Snygg I published the first outline for a phenomenological psychology in 1949.[3] It has since come to be known as Perceptual or Experiential Psychology because it seeks to understand persons and their behavior from the behaver's own perspective; that is to say, from the point of view of the person's own experience or perceptions of self and the world. I believe perceptual psychology provides a frame of reference sufficiently comprehensive to include the best contributions of behavioral psychology and extends beyond to incorporate modern humanistic thinking as well. I have found it most consistent with my own research and experience, most useful for providing effective guidelines for my professional practice and most compatible with other aspects of my personal theory of teaching.

Most American teachers are already well acquainted with the basic principles of behavioristic psychology. It is the psychology upon which most of our educational thinking has been based for several generations. Therefore, I shall not attempt to repeat those principles in this discussion; neither will I try to compress the whole of perceptual psychology into this chapter. That is the task of another volume.[4] In the remainder of this chapter I shall only attempt to sketch several concepts from perceptual psychology of special value for my personal theory of teaching.

The Relationship of Perception to Behavior

The basic concept of perceptual psychology is that all behavior is a consequence of the behavior's personal meanings or perceptions. In formal terms, the experiential psychologist states it, "All behavior, without exception, is a function of the perceptual field of the behaver at the instant of acting." In everyday terms this might be paraphrased, "We behave according to how things seem to us." This seems so obvious in our own experience that one may wonder why it is necessary to make a fuss about it. Every science, including the science of psychology, must begin with some fundamental assumption about its subject matter. Behavioral psychology assumes that behavior is a function of the stimulus. Traditional psychoanalysis assumes that behavior is a product of the id, ego, and super ego. Behavior modification assumes that behavior is a function of its consequents. Perceptual psychology takes personal meanings or perceptions as the origin of behavior and personality.

The basic assumption that behavior is a function of perception makes it possible to build an understanding of human behavior in *both* behavioral and experiential terms. For example, understanding behavior as a product of perception or personal meaning can improve the success of attempts to control specific behavior. Understanding that it is the *meaning* of the stimulus to the subject, the *meaning* of consequents to the behaver which determines responses, can help even the strictly behavioral psychologist refine techniques and achieve control of behavior with greater accuracy.

People behave according to their perceptions or personal meanings. That fact is immensely useful in helping us understand the behavior of other persons. I once watched a neighbor walk about in the field next to his house shaking weeds over his empty hat. Inquiring about his daft behavior, he reminded me that he was a science teacher and explained that he was collecting samples of pollen for students to examine under microscopes in his biology lab. Even the strangest, most puzzling behaviors of other people make sense when seen from their points of view. Failure to understand how others are perceiving is a primary cause of breakdowns in human communication.

The Perceptual Field

According to perceptual theory, the behavior of a person at any moment is the product of his or her perceptual field at that instant. What is meant by the "perceptual field" is all those perceptions or personal meanings existing for the person at the moment of acting. Though a person's behavior is always a function of the total field, not all perceptions have equal value or influence upon behavior. Let us take as an example the personal meanings I have as I sit at my desk writing these lines. Some of my perceptions are highly stable and I have them at almost every moment of my life. Among these are my perceptions of myself as Art Combs, male. Other fairly constant personal meanings are my values, long-term goals, and beliefs about many aspects of the world I live in. As I sit here writing I am also aware of my study, the yard outside my window, my typewriter, desk, and telephone, and many other familiar items on and around my desk. If I move from the study to my living room many of the perceptions in my field will give way to those in my new surroundings, while personal meanings about myself, my body condition, and most of my values and goals will remain the same. Wherever I am and whatever I am doing, however, my behavior is always a function of my total perceptual field at that moment.

One other aspect of the field needs mention. The perceptions determining behavior vary in degrees of clarity of sharpness. Meanings may be in figure or ground; that is to say, in sharp focus or so vague and indistinct that one may not be able to report them to some one else. At this moment, for example, my perceptions of the yard outside my window, the carpet on the floor, and the books on my bookshelves are part of the ground of my field. I am vaguely aware that they are there but they are not in the center of my attention. On the other hand, the keyboard of my typewriter is in very clear figure because, unfortunately, I am not a touch typist and must clearly perceive where I put my fingers in order to type this sentence. Events perceived in figure are sometimes called, *conscious* and those in ground, *unconscious*. Actually, perceptions are never one or the other. Rather, personal meanings may exist at any level of clarity from figure to ground and affect our behavior with consequent degrees of precision or vagueness.

Changing student perceptions or personal meanings is what teaching is all about. To do that well, requires teacher awareness of student perceptions and meanings. Research on good and poor teachers, for example, reveals that good teachers are strongly empathic.[5] That is to say, they have the capacity to put themselves in the student's shoes and perceive the world from the student's point of view. They are sensitive to how students think, feel, believe about themselves and others, and the situations in which they find themselves. Poor teachers, the research demonstrates, are primarily concerned with how things look to the teacher. Since people behave according to how things seem to them, effective teaching must begin with awareness of how students perceive and what affects the perceiving process.

IMPORTANT FACTORS DETERMINING PERCEPTION

Perceptual psychology provides a framework for understanding the nature and function of perceiving. Among the factors determining people's perceptions suggested by experiential psychology are the following.

The Physical Organism

How people perceive is affected by the bodies in which they travel about. The most obvious contributors to perceiving are, of course, our sense organs, those "windows on the world" which make it possible for us to be aware of what goes on about us. The possession and acuity of organs for hearing, vision, taste, smell, and touch play an important role in providing the raw data for many perceptions. Other less obvious aspects of our physical bodies also affect personal meaning. What people perceive, for example, may be greatly affected by height; tall people have a different perspective on the world from short ones. Physical condition and health may also have vital effects on perception by affecting alertness or determining where the body is located and hence what opportunities it is exposed to. A sick person lying in bed has a far different experience of the world than an active, perambulating, involved person. Personal perceptions may also be deeply affected by the reactions of others to our physical selves. In our society it is a helpful thing to be regarded as handsome, acceptable, and attractive. It is a very different experience to be regarded as homely, inadequate, or ugly.

Some Effects of Time on Perception

How people perceive is also affected by time. Generally speaking, the longer one is exposed to an opportunity, the more one is likely to perceive. The longer one stares at a carpet, for example, the greater the number of details come into figure. But time is important for perception in another way. Most of our perceptions are dependent, in one way or another, on previous ones. In mathematics, for example, one needs to know how to add before he or she can understand multiplication. Similarly, what choices teachers make about methods for use in a particular lesson will be dependent on much previous information and experience. Optimum speed for acquiring new perceptions varies widely from student to student and many a teacher has suffered defeat by failing to adjust to the importance of time in perceiving. Perception takes time—and too much haste, pressure, or impatience with the perceiving process can hinder or destroy an otherwise good learning experience for teachers and students alike. On the other hand, too slow an approach to learning may result in boredom, apathy, or desire to escape to more promising activities.

Opportunity and Perception

The personal meanings we possess are deeply affected by the opportunities we have had. Aboriginal tribes, for example, have quite different experiences from those of us who live in complex modern societies. Children raised in different families have different opportunities to perceive. Even children in the same families may have vastly different experiences from brothers or sisters. What one knows, thinks, feels, believes, comprehends, or even aspires to is determined in large part by the cultural environments and the significant persons we have interacted with in real or symbolic terms. Opportunity has always been an important factor in human perception, but the fabulous development of communication systems in the past several generations has increased human opportunities for perception by incredible amounts. Through radio, television, telephone, information storage, and retrieval systems people now have opportunities for perceiving as never before in all of human history.

Need and Perception

The effects of the physical body, time, and opportunity on perception are generally understood by most people. One less understood factor determining perception is need. In Chapter 2 I spoke of the fundamental need of all human beings to move toward health or fulfillment if they can. The operation of this basic need or its various expressions also has a selective effect on perceiving. Generally speaking, we tend to perceive those events related to the fulfillment of our need to maintain and enhance the self. One can observe numerous examples of this effect by a simple examination of personal behavior from moment to moment throughout the day. When we are thirsty, we become aware of the drinking fountain we have passed many times without notice. We become aware of the ads for new cars when our old one seems to be getting shabby. We select the right time to cross the street. We argue with someone who has disagreed with us. We perceive what is important or threatening to ourselves with great sharpness. What is not we are likely to forget, overlook, or misunderstand.

In daily life fundamental need is generally focused from moment to moment on more specific goals, objectives, or activities leading to maintenance and enhancement of self. Need for fulfillment might be expressed in action, for example, as a student seeks to make friends with another student, eat an apple, go to the bathroom, solve a problem, buy a dress, avoid a fight, sign up for football, etc. Obviously, such moment to moment expressions of need will also vary in significance to the student. The more fundamental an event seems for satisfying need in an individual, the more effect it will have in determining perceptions. Examples may be seen in the hierarchy of needs discussed by Maslow.[6] Human needs, he tells us, can be ordered in a five-step hierarchy as follows:

1 Physiological needs—for air, water, food, warmth.
2 Safety needs—for security, stability, freedom from fear and the like.
3 Belongingness and love needs—affectionate relationships with people and the feeling that one belongs in some social context.

4   Esteem needs—for achievement, adequacy, mastery, reputation, recognition, importance.
5   Self-actualization needs—for self-fulfillment, transcendence, or to actualize potential.

In this hierarchy people's basic needs must first be reasonably fulfilled before they can give much attention to higher level ones. Starving people, for example, are unlikely to give much thought to the fine points of democracy. Similarly, the child deeply worried about an impending divorce in the family is unlikely to be able to pay attention to highly abstract questions of grammer, history, or mathematics.

As we have seen in Chapter 2, the basic need for maintenance and enhancement exists in every cell and has its effect on every human action. It cannot be ignored. It is also immediate. Few of us are much motivated by far off satisfactions of need unless we can feel that remote satisfactions can be achieved through smaller steps to be taken now. This immediate nature of need creates many problems for education charged with the responsibility to prepare students for the future. It is a difficult task to convince students intent upon fulfilling immediate, personal needs that they ought to be working hard to learn this or that thing because "some day you will need it." In a later chapter I will discuss this dilemma of student and society needs in greater detail.

Values, Goals, and Techniques

In the course of growing up most of us come to differentiate guidelines for action as a consequence of our experiences with the world. These generalized selective factors are often called goals, values, or techniques. Such guidelines may also be positive or negative, goals or values to be sought or avoided. The basic need of one individual may find expression in such goals as getting married, being a farmer, getting a college degree. For another, satisfaction might be sought by remaining single, becoming a fisherman, avoiding further schooling, etc. Values are similar differentiations for satisfying need, but usually less concrete than goals. They are generalized concepts and have important selective effects upon perceptions.

So, different persons might value art, baseball, music, equal rights for women, the masculine role, and democratic values depending upon how these matters have contributed to the satisfaction of the person's need in the past. Once established, values thereafter exert important selective effects on other perceptions.

Techniques are also generalized concepts acquired from experience and exert selective effects upon the individual's perceptions. They have to do, however, with the methods persons have come to count upon for achieving need satisfaction. So some persons may seek fulfillment by throwing themselves into projects, others may seek to achieve their ends by the exertion of power, by weeping, guile, flattery, bribery, or any of thousands of other methods that have proven useful in the past.

Self-Concept and Perception

Among the most important concepts in perceptual psychology is the self-concept.[7] As we have seen, people behave according to their perceptions of themselves and the world about them. So at any moment a major factor in behavior is the beliefs we hold about ourselves. A vast literature now exists in psychology demonstrating how people's self-concepts affect every aspect of human activity. Here are some of the more important things we know about the self-concept and its effects on behavior.

What is the self-concept?   Each of us has thousands of perceptions about ourselves. We see ourselves as men, women, tennis players, Americans, fat or thin, smart or stupid, and many, many more. Some of our concepts of ourselves are very important to us, like our beliefs that we are male or female, for example. We have lived with those ideas all our lives and they have become integral and central aspects of our belief systems. They would be very difficult, if not impossible, to change. Other beliefs about ourselves are much less central and more open to change. For example, my concept of myself as the owner of a 79 VW could be changed very quickly if someone wished to buy me a newer model car. All of the thousands of ways in which a person sees himself or herself taken together compose the self-concept. It is the self we refer to when we speak of "I" or "me," the self we are forever seeking to maintain and enhance.

We acquire our self-concepts from life experiences, especially from interactions with the important people in our worlds. The self-concept is learned and, once in place, is often difficult to change. This is not to say that change is impossible. Despite its fundamental stability, many aspects of the self-concept may change throughout our lifetimes.

What the self-concept does.   A person's self is his or her most precious possession, the very center of all experience. Whatever is experienced is somehow related to the self. Things may be near or far, to the right or to the left, important or unimportant, attractive or repulsive to the self. But the self-concept is not only the center of our existence. It also exerts a continuous and crucial selective effect on everything else we see or do. We select our perceptions in terms of our self-concepts. One needs but to go shopping with a member of the opposite sex to discover very quickly how one's self-concept as man or woman determines what is looked at, responded to, liked, disliked, purchased, or ignored. People do what seems appropriate to their self-concepts. They avoid what seems out of line.

The possession of a particular concept of self also produces behavior that is likely to corroborate existing beliefs. So the person who wants to be liked but feels he or she is not may avoid other people or try too hard to attract their attention. Either way, that person's existing belief is supported because he or she avoids interacting with people or because "trying too hard" turns people off. The world is full of people who believe they are only X much. As a consequence that's all the much they do. Other people, seeing them behave so, conclude, "Well, that's an X much person" which only proves what the person believed in the first place! Millions of people are caught in such vicious circles, prisoners of their own perceptions. Many end up as serious social problems for the rest of us.

The effect of the self-concept can be seen in almost every aspect of human activities. Research has shown, for example, that the self-concept is a better predictor of a child's success in reading than intelligence scores.[8] Indeed, how intelligently a person is able to behave is, itself, a function of the self-concept. People who believe they can, will try. People who believe they cannot see no point in trying. The doers are regarded as intelligent, while the reluctant ones suffer by comparison.

Whether people are well or badly adjusted seems also to be a function of the self-concept. People who see themselves in positive ways, as liked, wanted, acceptable, able persons of dignity and integrity, behave so and, as a consequence, get along well in our society. The ones we have trouble with as children and who grow up to fill our jails and mental hospitals and institutions are the ones who see themselves in negative ways—unliked, unwanted, unacceptable, unable, unworthy. Dozens of studies attest to the fact that students who see themselves in positive ways learn better, and achieve greater excellence.[9] Even success in one's occupation seems largely dependent upon a person's belief about self. Researches seeking significant differences between effective and ineffective workers in such helping professions as counseling, teaching, pastoral care, even politics show effective workers have positive views of self while ineffective ones have negative views.[10]

To this point I have tried to state only the very basic premises of the perceptual way of looking at people and their behavior. In later chapters we will have an opportunity to explore the perceptual view of learning, human adjustment, and the bases of human interactions in greater detail. For now, however, let us examine some of the more significant implications perceptual concepts have for me as a professional educator.

IMPLICATIONS OF PERCEPTUAL THOUGHT FOR PRACTICE

If it is true that people behave according to their perceptions or personal meanings, then a prime requisite for working successfully with people must be an awareness of how things look from their points of view. This ability to put one's self in another's shoes is technically known as *empathy*. Humanistically oriented teachers more often call it *sensitivity*. By whatever name, understanding how things look to the students one works with is the place from which teaching must begin.

A number of researches on good and poor teachers have demonstrated that sensitivity or empathy is characteristic of highly effective teachers.[11] Effective teachers are continuously concerned about how things look from the points of view of their students. On the other hand, ineffective teachers are much less aware of how things look from the student's point of view. Instead, they base their activities on how things look to themselves. The goal of education is to produce some change in student personal meanings. Awareness of student perceptions, therefore, is necessary to determine whether educational processes have had any significant effect. Effective communication is the basic tool of the teaching profession. It is the primary vehicle through which the processes of education operate, but communication is dependent on common meanings in the perceptual fields of communicators, another reason why empathy is a necessity for effective teaching. Failure to understand how things look to others is a common cause for the breakdown of human communication whether we are talking about individuals or nations.

Some people have misunderstood the humanistic educator's concern for understanding how things seem to students. They conclude that such concentration must mean an accompanying lack of concern for excellence, failure to properly guide student activities, or a surrender of the teacher's own expertise. The emphasis of humanistic educators on sensitivity however is not simply a desire to be seen by students as warm, friendly, or caring. It is true that sensitive persons are very likely to be perceived by others in such ways, but humanists do not value such relationships simply because they want to coddle students or want people to like them. Humanists value sensitivity because through it they come in touch with the data required to carry out their professional responsibilities. Empathy or sensitivity does not require that I give up my own ways of perceiving. Quite the contrary. If I understand how things appear to students I am in closer touch with the realities of what is going on.

This not only helps me select activities for students; it also provides the information I need to communicate my own points of view with a greater probability of success.

Learning Sensitivity

Sensitivity or empathy is not a difficult skill to acquire. Children do it quite automatically with respect to grown-ups who surround them. It is a matter of survival for children to be aware of what powerful or important adults are thinking and feeling. Even as adults we never completely lose this skill. We are highly sensitive to our husbands, wives, lovers, bosses, supervisors, or anyone in a position to effect our need satisfactions in important ways. Developing sensitivity for the professional helper is not a question of learning something entirely new. It is only to apply what he or she already does with important persons to those in less powerful, more subservient positions. It is a matter of doing what one already knows how to do, only doing it professionally and systematically.

The process is a simple matter of reading behavior backwards. If it is true that people's behavior is a function of how they are perceiving, feeling, and believing, then, if we observe behavior carefully, we should be able to reconstruct the personal meanings that produced it. This is the process of inference used by professional counselors, teachers, social workers, and many others. Observing the behavior of students or clients, one asks, "Now how would a person have to feel or perceive to behave like that?" The answers to such questions provide hypotheses that can then be checked against other behaviors. Over a period of time, through a series of observations, inferences, and checks against further behavior, it is possible to develop clearer and clearer pictures of how other persons are thinking and perceiving.

To teach beginning counselors and teachers empathic skills, I have often found it useful to play the "Listening Game." This involves dividing students in small groups, even one to one, to talk about anything that deeply interests them with one additional requirement: That no one may speak until he or she has first repeated the gist of what the previous speaker tried to say in a way satisfactory to the previous speaker. At first this experience is highly frustrating because we do not ordinarily listen with such attention. However, with practice, one learns to become more sensitive to what others are trying to express, even to the personal meanings that lie behind the words they use. Psychologists sometimes call this "listening with the third ear."

The Immediate View of Behavior

A major contribution of perceptual psychology to the teaching-helping professions is its interpretation of human behavior from an immediate point of view. If it is true that behavior is a function of a person's perceptions, then the crucial causes of behavior are now, in the present. The importance of this idea for the processes of teaching can hardly be overestimated. For several generations teachers have been told they must know all about their students' pasts in order to deal effectively with them. An occasional elementary teacher with only twenty or thirty children in class may, by the end of the year, develop a fairly comprehensive understanding of the case histories of all his or her students. The task is practically impossible for the average high school teacher with several hundred flowing through the classroom everyday. I find the idea that students can be dealt with in the present, without full knowledge of their pasts, provides new hope and new possibilities for successful teaching.

The fact that behavior is a function of present perceptions does not deny the fact that we are all products of our past experience. Certainly past experience has deeply affected how we perceive in the present and *any* information about another person *can* be useful in helping toward better understanding of how that person is perceiving now, at this moment. Knowing how other people are thinking, feeling, believing, seeing can provide us with immediately useful clues to more effective action. The more accurate our understandings of a person's perceptual world, the more likely it is that we willl be able to create effective learning situations for that person.[12]

The fact that behavior is a function of present perceptions also means that it is possible to do something to help other persons even if we do not understand "how they got this way." Awareness of a student's current perceptual field often points to immediate
possibilities for treatment. A teacher who understands that a particular child feels unliked can find ways of helping such a child feel
better even if the teacher has no idea how the student came to feel
that way in the first place. Knowing the student feels unliked, at the
very least, a teacher can begin by making sure the child feels liked by
his teacher. After that, the teacher can find dozens of ways in any
classroom, laboratory, or playground situation to provide self-concept building experiences for a student. The immediate view of behavior provided by perceptual thinking provides new hope that there
is something we can do for any students, no matter what their past, if
we can properly understand how they are seeing themselves and
their world in the present. I find that fact immensely supporting and
encouraging in my professional life.

Time and the Physical Organism

Understanding the significance of time and the state of
the physical organism in perception has immensely improved my
teaching and at the same time made me less of an ogre to my students. There was a time when I tried to fill a lecture or a speech with
as many "important" points as I could squeeze in and held students
strictly accountable for being able to reproduce them on demand. I
know better now. I know it takes time to perceive new personal
meanings and if I can communicate two or three important ideas in a
single session, I feel I have done a good hour's work. I am no longer
obsessed with deadlines nor am I desperate to "cover the subject" in
a given period of time. As a result my students learn better. In addition, both they and I can approach our tasks and each other in more
relaxed fashion and with greater personal enjoyment.

In similar fashion my awareness of the effects of the
physical organism upon perception affects my teaching. At the
simplest level I am reminded of the old adage that "the mind can

absorb no more than the seat can endure" and I try to make the physical conditions for learning as pleasant as possible. In seeking the causes of learning difficulties the state of a student's health and vigor is one of the questions I raise with myself. My understanding of the importance of physical factors on perception has also caused me to join the millions of other Americans currently exploring personal health and fitness with a new enthusiasm and enjoyment. I have a new respect for my body and its relationship to other aspects of my life. I can experience for myself how much more I am alive, awake and eager to tackle events when my physical house is in order. I could wish the same for my students.

Some Implications of Opportunity

Understanding the importance of opportunity for perception affects my teaching in many ways. The most obvious has to do with an appreciation of the wide diversity of experience from which students come. No two are ever at the same state of readiness for whatever I have to offer. Experiences of the past have molded their perceptual worlds in unique and complex fashion. They come to me at all levels of sophistication from wide-eyed innocence to experience far wider, deeper, or more intense than my own. With such backgrounds, how can one treat them alike, or establish rigid rules and expectations?[13]

The need for understanding the prior experience of students is even greater with respect to students from ethnic or cultural backgrounds other than my own. I have only read about the street culture of our ghettos, have never been victim of a brutal father, or spent time "in stir." I have never suffered starvation, lived below the poverty level, or suffered the humiliation of being scorned and rejected for being different. Like thousands of my teacher colleagues, I grew up in comfortable, middle-class America. I have only heard about other folks' customs, traditions, and family life from friends and neighbors of other ethnic or cultural backgrounds. Though I have visited and worked in foreign countries with alternate ways of thinking and valuing, I do not really comprehend them like my students who have lived them. My students have not only had different opportunities for experience, they have often had better and richer ones. I cannot hope to understand the full flavor of this understanding and experience. I can make the effort, however, and even a small appreciation can improve the likelihood of my success at teaching. Even beyond my professional growth, I owe a great debt to the students I have known and the clients I have counseled for immeasurably adding to my own experience, values, and understanding. I am a better, more complete human being for it.

Unless I am sensitive to student perceptions, I cannot be sure what opportunities I am providing. With the best of intentions I have sometimes labored to plan and execute a beautiful lesson plan only to find it flop with a sickening thud when I put it into practice. The magnificent opportunity I thought I was creating turned out to be frustrating, unintelligible, inappropriate, inadequate, or just plain out of touch with where students were coming from. To create effective opportunities for learning for my students requires more than knowledge of my subject and good will. It requires continual monitoring of how my students are perceiving, and understanding where they are and what they are ready for next.

A Few Implications of Self-Concept for Practice

Our modern understanding of the self-concept and the dynamics of its effects upon people and their behavior is probably one of the most outstanding contributions of humanistic psychology. As indicated earlier, the self-concept is involved in every human experience, and educational processes are no exception. Since people behave in terms of their self-concepts, effective teaching requires a grasp of the ways students perceive themselves and their worlds when they come to me. It also means I must have some sort of belief about the kinds of self-concepts I want to foster. Understanding how students perceive themselves helps me comprehend even the most bizarre behavior. It also provides basic information for planning and creating effective learning experiences.

Even more important for my teaching is the fact that the self-concept is learned. People acquire their self-concepts from the ways in which they have been treated by the people surrounding them in the course of their growing up. This includes teachers. Schools do more than teach subjects. They teach people who they are and what they are as well. Students do not park their self-concepts at the classroom door. They bring their self-concepts with them wherever they go, and what happens to their beliefs about themselves may be a far more important learning experience than the particular curriculum to which they are being exposed.

All this requires:

1   That I be aware of the self-concepts of my students
2   That I recognize the possible significance of my own behavior upon the self-concepts of students
3   That the learning experiences I create make positive contributions to the self-concepts of students I work with.

To achieve those ends requires more than ability to see through the student's eyes which we have discussed in this chapter. It also demands that I possess some clear-cut ideas about the kinds of self-concepts schools ought to foster and full acceptance of responsibility for the impact of my own professional behavior on student self-concepts. I intend to return to those important questions in later chapters.

CHAPTER 4

Beliefs About Learning

Whatever one's theory about teaching, it must certainly include some conception of how people learn. Modern psychology offers us two broad approaches to understanding learning processes: a behavioral explanation and a perceptual-humanistic one. These are not mutually exclusive points of view. One is not wrong and the other right. Rather, each is especially useful for certain types of problems and one needs to include both frames of reference in a comprehensive personal theory. A professional worker with two tools at his or her command is better equipped than a worker with only one. Accordingly, both behavioral and perceptual concepts have a place in my personal theory.

THE BEHAVIORAL VIEW

Almost everyone has heard of the classic experiment of Pavlov who conditioned his dogs to salivate at the ringing of a bell just as they would when presented a piece of meat. This substitution of a new stimulus for an old one or the attachment of a new response to an old stimulus is called conditioning, and represents the basic process involved in learning according to behavioral thought. Beginning from this basic premise, behavioral psychologists have completed hundreds of researches on learning and have compiled an enormous literature illuminating every aspect of this conception. They have also provided many new concepts bearing upon the processes of learning. Among these are the principles of extinction, the fading or disappearance of an established response; generalization, spread of responses to other stimuli; reinforcement, strengthening of a given response by further stimulation or some form of reward.

In more recent years a branch of behaviorism, called Behavior Modification, has concentrated attention on learning as a function of the consequents of behavior rather than antecedent stimuli. People learn, "Behavior mod" workers point out, when a new behavior provides the learner with some sort of satisfaction or fulfillment. This group of psychologists has also expressed much doubt about the usefulness of punishment in learning. They recommend instead the reinforcement of desirable behaviors through assuring some sort of positive satisfactions for the learner. Behavior modification workers have also been deeply interested in educational research and have adapted many of their basic principles to the solution of classroom problems.[1]

A behavior modification approach to learning, I have found, is primarily useful for managing behavior or when applied to learning situations which can be precisely defined in specific behavioral terms. To use it effectively requires careful analysis of learning tasks and the establishment of clear-cut objectives in the simplest possible terms. One begins with a clear conception of the desired behavior, then analyzes the learning situation seeking ways to reinforce the desired behavior in as many ways as possible. One ignores contrary or extraneous behaviors and concentrates attention upon reinforcing desired ones. Teachers may also seek ways to bring desired behaviors into the learning arena so that they can be reinforced when they occur. Reinforcements can be of many varieties depending upon what is likely to have value in the eyes of the student. Reinforcement might be activated through some form of tangible reward. It might also be implemented in some form of teacher or peer approval, pleasure in achievement, or the like.

Sometimes undesirable behaviors can also be extinguished through the application of some form of negative consequents. Behavior modification theorists, however, do not recommend the use of punishment in classrooms largely because its usefulness is limited primarily to teaching people what *not* to do and because the use of punishment is often accompanied by side effects over which the teacher has little or no control.[2]

Behavioral approaches to learning are often useful in elementary grades for teaching children specific basic skills or for teachers whose subject matter fields lend themselves to precise behavioral definitions. As student maturity grows, as subject matter becomes more complex and educational goals more general, behavioral thinking is less and less useful for the guidance of practice and perceptual-humanist concepts have greater and greater relevance.

THE PERCEPTUAL VIEW OF LEARNING

A perceptual view of learning, like behavioral approaches, seeks to produce some change in the behavior of the learner. However, it regards behavior only as symptom of what is going on in the learner's perceptual field. Personal meanings or perceptions are regarded as the determiners of behavior. Learning, in this frame of reference, is regarded as the discovery of personal meaning.[3]

The basic principle has been expressed as follows: Any information or experience will affect a person's behavior only in the degree to which the person has discovered the personal meaning of that information for him or her. Here is an example to illustrate: Glancing through your local paper you find a statistical statement of disorders treated in your local hospital during the past year. As you flick your eyes over the tables, you read "Pulmonic stenosis, 50 cases." If you are like most people you probably do not know what pulmonic stenosis is and this information has no effect on your behavior whatever. It is just another of those millions of perceptions that drift through consciousness, "in one ear and out the other" as the saying goes. Several days later one of your friends casually mentions the term in the course of a conversation. Now the matter has a little more meaning to you. It is something your friend knows about and you don't. Accordingly, you go to a dictionary and look it up.

You find it is a congenital heart defect involving the closing of the pulmonary artery often requiring heart surgery to repair the condition when a child reaches puberty. Later in the week you receive a letter from the mother of one of the children in your class. She says, "We have just returned from a trip to the clinic where Elaine was examined on Friday. She has a heart condition which will require surgery next year. Meantime, we need to keep an eye on her and be sure she does not overexert herself. We would appreciate your help in this." The concept now has more meaning to you. It is happening to one of your students. You assure the mother of your cooperation. You talk to your colleagues about Elaine and you keep an eye on her in your class and on the playground. She is much in your thoughts. Now, let us go one step further. Suppose you have just learned that your own young child suffers from this condition. What then? The concept now affects your thinking tremendously. It intrudes into everything you do and affects a large proportion of your time and energies. The closer events are perceived to ourselves, the more vitally they affect our behavior. Learning, according to perceptual psychology, is essentially a problem in the personal discovery of meaning.

The perceptual view of learning has sometimes been called *experiential learning* for it concentrates attention upon the experience of the learner. A few of the basic principles affecting perceptual-experiential learning of special relevance for teachers are:

1   Learning is a deeply personal experience.
2   It is motivated by personal need.
3   It is critically affected by the learner's concepts of self.
4   The learner's experience of challenge and threat determines degrees of involvement.
5   It is deeply influenced by the learner's experience of identification or belonging.
6   Meaningful feedback or knowledge of results is required.

1   Learning is a deeply personal process.   Truly effective learning is much more than the acquisition of information or simple skills. It is a deeply personal activity having to do with people's feelings, attitudes, beliefs, understandings, and values. It is an affective as well as a cognitive experience. A closer look at the nature of emotion will help to understand the vital role of human feelings in the learning process.

Psychologically, emotion is understood as a state of readiness or acceleration. It plays an important part in getting the organism ready for action. Asleep, the organism needs very little energy to operate. Like an automobile with its engine idling, body acceleration is then very low. As a person wakes up and begins to go about the day's affairs, more activity is required and body processes are speeded up to meet the new requirement—pulse rates increase, body tone is heightened, breathing quickens, etc. If the person perceives an important source of satisfaction or danger to self, the tempo rises still further, accompanied by speeding up of some body processes (breathing becomes more rapid, blood pressure rises) and slowing down of others (digestion slows or stops). This puts the organism on a "ready for action" basis, prepared to deal with the crisis, either to encounter or flee. When the importance of events to self is very high, as in the case of serious threat or ecstasy, acceleration may be so great that the person may be "frozen," "stage struck," "shocked," or immobilized, like an automobile with its engine racing and the brakes full on. The more important or threatening events seem to the self, the stronger is the excitement or emotion experienced.

The person's description of internal states associated with emotion is usually expressed as "feeling." So we speak of feeling afraid, angry, loving, or hating depending upon the objects with which our experiences of emotion are associated. Feelings are really shorthand descriptions of experience at the moment of their occurrence. Rarely do they convey the full import of what is experienced, but they represent the best we can manage to communicate about the very complex and personal perceptions we experience.

Referring to the illustration of learning in the previous section, we can see how emotion increases as the event comes closer to self. Pulmonic stenosis as a statistic affects us not at all. Mentioned by an acquaintance, minor feelings are aroused. Referring to one of our students affects us more, perhaps with anxiety or concern. Discovering that it applies to our own child is likely to be devastating. The degree of emotion experienced thus serves as a rough indicator of the relevance of events to the person's self.

If learning is the discovery of personal meaning, and emotion is an indicator of the degree of that meaning, it follows that learning must be understood as a deeply personal, emotional experience as well as a cognitive one. Learning is not a mere matter of acquiring skill or a body of information. It is also a question of feelings, attitudes, beliefs, values, and emotional experience. The greater the degree of emotion the more likely it is that learning is important to the learner and so will affect behavior. In this sense, arguments over whether education ought to be "affective" or not are nonsense. If education is not affective, then very little of any consequence has occurred.

2   Personal need and learning.   As we have seen in Chapter 2 all behavior is motivated by the basic need of the organism for self fulfillment. This includes the processes of learning. Of all the factors known to affect learning, the effect of need is among the most certain. Even in learning experiments with rats it is customary to make certain the rat is hungry so that it has need to search for food. The effect of need is present in all aspects of learning. People learn best when they have a need to know.

People work very hard at learning when they have a need to know and when they believe they have a chance of success. Students studying a foreign language in American schools laboriously plug away at the task. The same students set down in a foreign country out of touch with English speaking friends and acquaintances, quickly pick up the language because it is no longer just a subject to be learned, but a necessity for effective living. At any moment each of us does what it seems we must to achieve adequacy and fulfillment. People do what seems to them important. They ignore what seems unimportant or irrelevant. When forced to confront matters that do not seem important, people respond with reluctance, apathy, or violence depending upon the degree of pressure they experience.

In the course of growing up each person discovers that his or her basic need can be achieved or hindered by various kinds of experiences. As a consequence, goals become differentiated to be sought or avoided; techniques for seeking fulfillment become defined as useful or damaging; and the basic need of an individual becomes operative in highly personal, individual ways. Some goals and techniques through which we seek fulfillment may be similar to those of people around us. Others will be purely our own. Many people become teachers, for example, because that occupation seems to them fulfilling. The goals they choose for achieving that fulfillment in the daily operation of their professional responsibilities, however, may be so diverse and personal as to defy classification.

3 The self-concept in learning. In Chapter 3 I outlined briefly some of the effects of self-concept on behavior. The self-concept is equally important in its implications for learning. Earlier in this chapter we observed that learning is a matter of the personal discovery of the meaning of events to self. The discovery of the relationship of ideas to self is crucial. Without relevance to self there is little personal meaning and little significant learning.

There are other ways in which the self-concept affects learning. People behave in terms of their self-concepts. Students who feel they are able to learn are likely to try. Students who do not feel able can be counted on to find ways of avoiding learning to escape embarrassment, humiliation, or fear. People who believe they can read, write, figure, or have good ideas approach learning tasks with interest or excitement. Students with opposite concepts of themselves and their abilities are likely to avoid such confrontations by running away from them physically, intellectually, or emotionally. What teacher is not familiar with the student whose body is there in class but whose attention is long gone or lost in a more satisfying world of imagination? People tend to live up to their expectations and the self-concept is a prime determiner of the attitudes with which people approach learning tasks and the amounts of effort they invest.

There is a second reason for concern about self-concept in learning. A person's self-concept is vital to growth, citizenship, and success in all walks of life. Self-concepts of students are important in their own right. We know that negative self-concepts are destructive to human personality, effective citizenship, and successful living while positive self-concepts are characteristic of intelligent, well adjusted, successful human beings. So, even if student self-concepts had no effect on learning whatever, schools and teachers would need to make the development of positive self-concepts an important goal of the curriculum and recognize that student self-concepts are being affected no matter what else the student may or may not be learning at any moment.

Self-concepts are learned. Schools therefore must be concerned with what students learn about themselves in school and out. Positive views of self are not only important for learning algebra, reading, chemistry, or philosophy. Positive views of self are important because they are factors in student growth and development, the very reason for a school's existence in the first place.

4   Challenge and threat in learning.   A fourth factor in perceptual approaches to learning has to do with the effects of challenge and threat. Effective learning requires getting involved. Whether and how people get involved is determined in large part by the person's experience of challenge or threat in the learning situation.

Psychologists tell us, and we can observe in our own experience, that people feel challenged when confronted with problems that interest them and which they believe they can handle successfully. People feel threatened, on the other hand, when they are confronted with problems they do not feel able to cope with successfully. Understanding these dynamics is important for teaching. For effective involvement in learning students need to feel challenged rather than threatened.

Whether people feel challenged or threatened, however, is not a matter of what the teacher believes is happening. It is how the student perceives of self and situations that count. With the best of intentions a teacher may believe he or she is challenging students while actually threatening the daylights out of them.

Whether students feel challenged or threatened is a question of how things seem to them, not how they seem to an outsider.

The importance of challenge or threat for learning is further underlined by two important effects of threat on human experience. Threat forces people to defend themselves or their existing positions. Everyone is familiar with this reaction. In the face of an attack or threat, we "get our backs up," and "dig in our heels." We resist threat by maintaining our existing positions or retreating to more defensible ones. Nobody wins an argument. The hotter the argument gets, the greater the vigor with which we defend our existing positions. Clearly such resistance to change and defense of existing positions is directly contrary to everything we are trying to do in encouraging learning. Learning requires change and whatever causes students to avoid or defend against change must surely be antithetic to the goals of teaching.

The second effect of threat is called "tunnel vision." This is a name psychologists have given to the experience under threat in which abilities to perceive become narrowed down to the object of threat while peripheral events are obscured. Anyone who has ever had the experience of being deeply threatened can recall how sharply the source of danger was perceived and how other events faded into the background or were not perceived at all. These dynamics may even occur when we are only mildly threatened as in the case of some anxiety that keeps popping back into our awareness over and over in the course of a day. Under threat perception becomes riveted upon the threatening object, like looking through a tunnel, and accompanying events may not be perceived at all. This tunnel vision effect of threat is also antithetic to what we are trying to do in teaching. We do not want students' perceptions to be narrowed. The purpose of education is to broaden perception, to open student awareness.

Effective learning calls for challenging students without threatening them. To accomplish this requires awareness of how things are in the perceptual world of students. Teachers must be able to see through student eyes, be sensitive enough to student experience to judge whether students are being challenged or threatened. With that understanding they can then adjust teaching strategies to maximize challenge and minimize threat and so effectively motivate students for further learning.

5   Identification or belonging in learning.   A fifth human factor in learning has to do with the feeling of oneness or belonging. Each of us in the process of growing up learns to identify or feel "one with" significant people around us. As infants we come to feel one with our parents, brothers, sisters, aunts, uncles, and children in the neighborhood. Later on we come to identify with "my school," "my state," "my nation," "my world," perhaps even the universe itself. Some of these feelings of oneness or identification with others may be so strong that we speak of them as love. Some people, unhappily, never get very far in the cycle of belonging. They get side tracked along the way. They feel identified only with the white ones but not the black ones, the Arabs but not the Israelis, Americans but not the Russians and so on.

Feelings of identification or belonging come about as a consequence of being cared for by those who surround us in the process of growing up. Such feelings are important factors in the personal development of every individual. Well adjusted, self-actualizing, successful persons have deep feelings of identification or belonging with large numbers of human beings. They speak of a feeling of "oneness in the human condition." Maladjusted, unhappy persons, on the other hand, are often characterized by deep feelings of alienation, deprivation, and convictions that "nobody cares." Feelings of identification and belonging are characteristic of self-actualization and success. They also have extremely important implications for learning.

People learn best when they have a feeling they are cared for and belong. David Aspy and Flora Roebuck, in a book titled, *Kids Don't Learn From Teachers They Don't Like,* have documented this principle with a whole series of researches demonstrating that students learn more quickly and effectively in a setting where they are cared for by their teachers.[4] Feelings of oneness and belonging are stimulating and encouraging. They give students strength to try and create desires to learn what others around them are interested in.

To gain a personal feeling of the effects of identification and belonging on the processes of learning one needs only to review one's own experience. Ask yourself how you feel when you are loved, when you feel you belong or are "one with" the important people in your life. Here are some of the words you probably use to describe your experience: excited, exhilarated, active, stimulated, interested, wanting to be involved. Now ask yourself, what kinds of feelings do you have when you experience alienation, rejection, being an outsider? If you are like most people, I suspect you describe your feelings in such terms as: dull, despair, apathy, indifference, depression, and you want to avoid humiliation, embarrassment, or pain. If the feeling of alienation is very great you may even feel a desire to revolt or to punish those from whom you feel excluded. Clearly the feelings accompanying belonging, identification, and caring are constructive and stimulating to learning. Those accompanying alienation are destructive not only to an individual's learning but are very likely to result in behavior that destroys or impedes the learning of others as well. After all, if one does not feel he or she is a member of the club there is no reason why one should pay his or her dues or look out for the other members.

6 Feedback in learning. If learning is understood as the personal discovery of meaning, it follows that learners need to be continuously aware about where they are and where they need to go next. This calls for some kind of feedback or knowledge of results with respect to the student's performance. But what should this feedback or evaluation be like?

From the principles about learning stated so far we can extract a number of criteria for providing feedback likely to stimulate and encourage student learning. Feedback, it seems clear, should be:

1 Immediate. Learning is directly affected by the perceived relationship to self. The closer the event to self, the more powerful the motivating effect. Innumerable experiments on conditioning and behavior modification have demonstrated that the motivating power of consequents rapidly decreases with the elapse of time from the behavioral incident. Most potent motivations are immediate ones. For maximal motivation, therefore, feedback or evaluation should occur as soon after the event as possible.

2 *Personal.*   For maximal effect feedback or evaluation should be personal. What the learner needs to know continuously is where he or she is, what is the outcome of actions just completed, and what needs to be done next. This is highly personal data quite unrelated to what others may be doing. Comparative data locates the learner with respect to others. It sheds no light on where he or she is with respect to self and contributes nothing at all to comprehension of what the learner just did or where to go next. Comparison with others puts a label on the learner: better—average—worse. Such labels may encourage or discourage the learner's efforts, but they have the effect of diverting attention away from achievement of the task to concern for standing as a competitor.

3 *Challenging rather than threatening.*   To provide effective motivation, feedback, or evaluation must be challenging rather than threatening. As we have already seen, people feel challenged by problems that interest them and which seem to them they have a chance of being successful with. People feel threatened when they do not feel able to cope with problems. These principles also apply to feedback and evaluation. People are motivated by challenge. They are turned off by threat.

4 *Relevant to the task.*   For effective motivation, feedback should concentrate the learner's attention on the task itself. The locus of satisfaction for learning should be in the accomplishment. Learning for some extraneous or artificially contrived reward distracts the learner from the main task and is very likely to result in only temporary learning. Who has not studied hard to learn some unimportant or uninteresting topic in order to

get a good grade, to avoid failure, or to fulfill a requirement only to find the material was quickly forgotten when the extraneous goal was achieved? For many years in the course of my teaching I frequently employed such comments as, "I like that," That's good!" or "I'm proud of you." In more recent years I have come to recognize that such motivating comments place the locus of student satisfaction in pleasing me rather than in the achievement itself. Accordingly, in more recent years I find myself more often using such phrases as, "Wow! I'll bet that makes you feel good," "Gee! Last week you couldn't do that," "It makes you feel good to do that, doesn't it?" or "Now that you know how to do that, perhaps you would like to help Fred."

5 **Point the way to next steps.** If possible effective feedback should do more than simply report to the student where he or she is. If it can help the learner perceive what needs to come next, the motivating effect can be immensely enhanced. This is another reason why feedback should be related to the task itself. Satisfactions inherent in the matter being learned are more likely to contain clues for next steps, suggest hypotheses to be explored, mistakes to be corrected. Giving a student an A for work on a project says only, "Your instructor approves of what you did." A statement like, "I guess you feel good about that," "You are very near the end," or "What do you think you need to do next?" is much more likely to be relevant and helpful to the student.[5]

SOME GENERAL IMPLICATIONS FOR PROFESSIONAL TEACHING

Generally speaking, I find the traditional S-R and behavior modification approaches to learning are especially useful when desired behaviors can be precisely defined, as in the case of teaching a skill like writing, simple arithmetic, or learning how to behave in class. When stimuli and consequents can be clearly discerned and controlled, behavioral concepts of learning can be very helpful and I do not hesitate to use them when they are applicable. No doubt elementary teachers or remedial education teachers responsible for teaching of basic skills would find them much more relevant than I.

A great deal of my teaching is concerned with broad holistic objectives like good citizenship, mental health, intelligent behavior, effective problem solving or some form of creative activity. Such goals do not lend themselves to precise behavioral definitions so I turn to perceptual-humanistic thinking for appropriate guidelines. Understanding learning as the personal discovery of meaning and understanding effects of need, self-concept, and identification are all helpful in creating and maintaining good learning encounters for my students. They are not only helpful in strategy—planning learning activities in advance—they are also useful in guiding my behavior in moment to moment decisions as I interact with students in the classroom, when I have to make instantaneous reactions to unforeseen events or take advantage of a momentary opportunity to explore new connections or wider implications.

Perceptual-humanistic theory also provides guidelines for me when the goal of learning is growth or change in student feelings, attitudes, beliefs, understandings, values, hopes, and aspirations. Behavioral approaches are not much help in these circumstances because there may be no observable behavioral outcomes or outcomes may be so unique as to defy prediction. To deal effectively with the inner life of student feelings, values, etc., calls for a perceptual orientation that can help me understand "where the student is coming from" and provide proper bases for my own responses to his or her current status and next steps.

A third area in which perceptual-humanistic thinking provides special help is when the goals of learning are not clear either to me or the student. Much of my work with students involves learning about things neither the student or I know about in advance. Together we are seeking solutions to some problem that interests us but neither has the answer when we start. Such circumstances require a conception of learning more concerned with creating processes for effective learning than arriving at "right" answers.

Two Tools or One?

In some quarters it is fashionable to argue over the superiority of behavioral or perceptual points of view of learning. These debates have been known to become very heated with each camp stoutly defending a chosen position and attacking the other. I think this is a great pity. It seriously inteferes with understanding and progress. I do not regard these concepts of learning as mutually exclusive. Rather, I see them as complementary with behavioral views making their main contributions when goals are clear, precise, and easily within control of the teacher. Perceptual-humanistic approaches have special relevance when goals are broader, when ultimate outcomes cannot be presently discerned or occur in the learner's personal world of thinking and feeling. For me, behavioral views may be incorporated within a larger perceptual-humanistic framework, but both points of view may be active in whatever task I am trying to facilitate. Operating in the perceptual orientation, I am frequently reinforcing student self-perceptions or ways of approaching questions. By ignoring many student behaviors I am contributing to their extinction. I may even help students to generalize their perceptions. On the other hand, when I am seeking specific behavioral outcomes, I may also be trying to understand how things look from the point of view of the student so that my reinforcements of behavior can be more precise and effective.

Information and Personal Meaning

The views of learning outlined in the previous pages have been immensely helpful to me in many ways. For one thing, they have provided a perspective from which I can understand the successes and failures of traditional education with greater clarity. They also provide important clues for ways in which some of our most pressing problems can be solved more effectively.

Learning as we have seen, has to do with student discovery of personal meaning. Teaching, then must be concerned with two basic processes: (1) helping students confront new information or experience, and (2) helping students discover personal meaning. Most teachers are expert at the first of these factors, providing information. This is the thing we have been doing for generations. Nowadays, with all our new techniques for transmitting information—television, radio, computers, audio-visual equipment, information retrieval systems—we can do it better than ever. We can provide students with more information, faster, more dramatically, and in more immediately useable form than ever before in history. Alas, we have not done nearly so well with the second half of the problem, finding ways to facilitate student discovery of the personal meaning of information. This seems a primary source of our failures.

Our historic preoccupation with the information or experience half of the learning equation, it seems to me, has led to two very unfortunate basic assumptions. One goes like this: Because I taught it, it was (or should have been) learned; therefore, there is no need to repeat it. This assumption is responsible for all sorts of mischief, and hard feelings among and failure of students to learn. It leads to the belief that there are specific levels on which particular learnings should take place. As a consequence teachers develop feelings of territory over subject matter and become incensed if others encroach on their turf. Schools are organized in grade levels and curricula are assigned to their "proper" places. Parents are discouraged from teaching children at home. Teachers who get out of line by teaching content out of the established phase are castigated for upsetting the prescribed order and sequence. Repeating content becomes a matter for disgrace. Teachers are shocked that pupils did not "get that in third grade" or whenever, and students are made to feel guilty for wanting to explore materials a second time.

The other assumption is that people aren't learning unless they are getting some new information. As a consequence, the obvious solution when students don't seem to have learned is to give them more, more, and more. Students, for their part, try hard to learn all this subject matter because they believe their teachers know what they are doing and this is "the way it's supposed to be." They take the information as best they can and breathe a sigh of relief when they can hang on to it long enough to dump it on the exams. As a matter of fact, many of our most important learnings have nothing to do with new information. They come about as a consequence of deeper and deeper exploration of ideas we already have. Few of us need more information about such principles as human brotherhood, personal honesty, human dignity, justice, or the elimination of prejudice. What we need is time, opportunity, and the disposition to explore the significance of such ideas for our selves and our relationships with others. It is the personal meaning of ideas that determines whether or not they are truly learned or are likely to affect behavior. When education falters, it is rarely because schools don't have information or teachers can't deliver it. School drop outs, for example, do not drop out because we didn't tell them; they never discovered the meaning of what schools had to offer.

It seems to me that perceptual-humanistic thinking about learning provides important clues to how we may begin to solve this dilemma. Its concentration on what is happening in the perceptual world of the learner helps me understand the processes determining the discovery of personal meaning and some of the conditions required for its encouragement and facilitation. It provides new maps for dealing with the very aspects of learning with which we have, historically, been least successful. This seems to me a valuable contribution to educational thought and has provided me with important guide lines for thinking about and experimenting with the ways I go about teaching.

Learning Is Personal and Subjective

If learning is personal and affective as perceptual theory suggests, then teaching must also be individual and subjective. Learning must be individual because people are unique and learning is personal. This is not to say that people cannot learn in group situations. Of course, they can and do. No matter how learners are organized, however, in the final analysis learning occurs only as individuals change their meanings or acquire new ones. This is true whatever the setting. Recognition of the personal, individual character of learning must be in the forefront of a teacher's planning.

Ever since the beginning of American education, schools have searched for ways to ignore or minimize the individual character of learning. To solve the problems of mass education all kinds of groupings have been employed to minimize individual differences and to find ways of teaching students alike. The effort continues to fail. Nevertheless, we continue to organize our schools in grade levels and tracks. We group children according to age, sex, race, IQ, reading, behavior adjustment, or any of a dozen other characteristics. Each generation keeps hoping its ways of grouping will produce better learning. Meantime, research on grouping continues to show that no method of grouping can be found to be superior for stimulating learning to any other method of grouping or even to no grouping at all.[6] Grouping in itself, is only an administrative expedient and has little or nothing to do with effective learning.

This is not to say that grouping is undesirable. An administrative expedient may contribute to convenience in handling large numbers of students and that may be a worthwhile contribution to a teacher's day. Problems arise, however, when expedience is confused with forwarding learning. There is no such thing as group learning. Learning is always individual no matter how students are organized. I am a firm believer in the values of group discussion and student interaction, and most of my teaching involves organizing students into groups of one kind or another for this purpose. I am aware, however, that it is the involvement in discussion and the dynamics of interacting which advances learning, not the fact of grouping or basis on which it was done. It is the student's individual and personal exploration and discovery of meaning that is crucial.

Since learning is personal and subjective, it seems to me effective teaching must also recognize and use the facilitative contributions of feeling and emotion in the classroom. The idea that learning is a cold, calculating, solely intellectual or cognitive function is destructive.[7] In some places enlightened educators who advocate affective education have been met with great opposition from persons who honestly believe attitudes, feelings, and values are outside the school's responsibility. They interpret concern for values in the public schools as blatant attempts to indoctrinate youth. They believe values, attitudes, and human beliefs are the proper responsibility of the home or the church and schools that foster humanistic education are messing around in matters that are none of their business. If it is true that learning is personal and affective, I see no alternative but for all of us in professional education to accept that fact and to construct learning experiences accordingly. I must welcome the exploration of feeling in students, encourage it, and demonstrate that I value such exploration in my classes. Anything less is to deny a fundamental principle of learning. Even if feeling and emotion were not so important a factor in learning as research has demonstrated, I would still value it in teaching simply because life is better that way. People cannot live and work effectively in cold, calculating, sterile environments. People need people. Wherever people interact, they do so on the basis of feelings, beliefs, attitudes, and values. I cannot conceive of teaching without such human qualities playing an important part in the process.

The Teacher's Role

The concept of learning we have been discussing also seems to me to call for a different conception of the teacher's role. Historically, teachers were regarded primarily as information providers. They were often the best informed persons in town, at least about academic matters. Teachers were expected to give people information or transmit knowledge, and teaching skills generally concentrated on lecturing, demonstrating, declaiming, telling, etc. But times have changed. Today there is so much more information available that no single human being can hope to possess even a very small portion of what is available. In addition, we now have a whole new array of techniques for gathering, classifying, analyzing, dramatizing, and presenting information through television, radio, computers, libraries, newspapers, books, and all manner of audio-visual devices. All these devices can provide vast quantities of information faster, more accurately, and certainly with more drama and appeal than the average teacher. They have made the teacher as a giver of information obsolete.

Another way of looking at teachers is to see them as "makers," "forcers," or "manipulators" of knowledge and students.

But teachers cannot *make* people learn. Learning occurs in people's perceptions. It goes on inside people and cannot be directly manipulated or controlled by outsiders. We have seen earlier that threat forces self-defense and tunnel vision, and behavior modification experts decry the use of punishment for learning. So the concept of teacher as maker and manipulator is unlikely to be very effective.

In most dictionaries teaching is defined as instructing, imparting knowledge or skill, to make to know, to show, guide, direct. Thinking about teaching in these terms led Carl Rogers to the conclusion that "teaching, in my estimation, is a vastly overrated function."[8] I agree. The role of the teacher as "teller" is outmoded. It is no longer enough. There is, however, a new role for the teacher called for by the concepts of learning and motivation we have been exploring in this chapter. For me, that new role makes teaching a truly professional occupation capable of making a significant contribution to my fellow human beings and the world I live in. It also provides me excitement, personal fulfillment, and a feeling of being a part of something much greater than self.

The Teacher as Facilitator

Learning and growth come about through the personal discovery of meaning. This is a process going on inside people and cannot be directly manipulated or controlled. It can, however, be encouraged and facilitated by the kinds of interactions people have with the outside world. We have also seen in Chapter 2 how the basic need of the organism for fulfillment impells the person toward growth if he or she can perceive that the way to fulfillment is open. People can, will, *must* move toward health *if* the way seems open to do so. The road to good teaching has to do with the big "if." Teaching is a process of creating conditions so the basic striving of the organism can do its thing. It is a process of encouraging, facilitating, and helping persons grow and discover personal meaning. Good teachers are not makers and molders. They are skillful helpers, aids, assistants or facilitators, ministers to the organism's own basic need. Teaching is a helping profession.

This is not to suggest that teacher personality or knowledge is unimportant. How effectively teachers facilitate will, of course, be deeply influenced by the teacher's personality and understandings. There is a vast difference, however, between using one's expertise to lay knowledge on students and using one's self as an effective instrument to facilitate learning. Teachers ought to be knowledgeable. That goes without saying. Teacher effectiveness, however, is not a function of a teacher's authority or expertise in a chosen field. It is a function of how teachers use themselves to help students discover personal meaning about themselves and the world they inhabit. Information can be conveyed by machine. The skillful use of self and the creation of conditions for significant learning is a truly professional achievement.

CHAPTER 5

More About Learning

In each chapter of this book I have tried to set down basic principles from some aspect of my personal theory of teaching and followed that with discussion of the implications of those concepts for my professional practice. For the most part, that plan has resulted in chapters of digestible length. The principles of learning I stated in Chapter 4, however, have so many important implications for teaching that I need a second chapter to deal with them properly. This chapter is therefore devoted to further implications of the fundamental principles of learning explored in Chapter 4.

To translate the principles of learning from my personal theory into practice, I find it helpful to think in terms of three phases of the learning process:

1. Creating the atmosphere for learning
2. Providing information or experience
3. Aiding discovery of meaning.

CREATING THE ATMOSPHERE
FOR LEARNING

The personal discovery of meaning cannot occur without the active participation of the learner. Therefore, the first step in teaching must be the creation of conditions that make involvement and participation possible. This is not always easy for the past experience of many students has made them leary of involvement in situations wherein their selves may be endangered. People who have been hurt learn highly ingenious ways for keeping their precious selves intact, free from deprecation or insult. Nor do they eagerly participate in events that do not seem likely to contribute to self-enhancement. The first step to effective teaching must be the creation of atmospheres for learning that encourage and facilitate involvement.

In recent years the helping professions have learned a great deal about atmospheres conducive to effective learning and change. A number of research studies have helped us become aware of the characteristics of teachers and relationships likely to result in productive atmospheres for learning. Among these are studies, designed to explore the characteristics of good and poor professional helpers, which have shown the importance of teacher or counselor abilities to be empathic, sensitive, and authentic in establishing facilitative atmospheres for learning and growth.[1] Carl Rogers postulated three "necessary and sufficient conditions" for effective helping relationships: empathic understanding, unconditional positive regard for the student or client, and "congruence"—counselor-teacher genuineness or accuracy of response to students or clients.[2] A whole series of researches designed to test these postulates in counseling have clearly demonstrated that they are, indeed, important essentials for helping relationships. The same characteristics have also been studied in the classroom by Aspy and Roebuck for several thousand hours of instruction. They find the teacher's realness, respect for students, and teacher awareness of the meaning of classroom experience for students to be closely associated with effective learning. Such facilitation characteristics were also associated with improved problem solving, more positive student self-concepts, fewer discipline problems, lower rates of absence from school, and even increases in intelligence![3]

Important clues for the creation of effective atmospheres for learning can also be found in four of the factors affecting learning stated in the previous chapter. For example, atmospheres need to be related to student need satisfaction. They ought to be conducive to positive self-concepts. They ought to be challenging without being threatening. And they ought to provide students with feelings of belonging and identification. All these provide me important clues for the creation of facilitating atmospheres for learning and I try to put them to work as I think and plan for teaching.

In the final analysis, what is happening in the classroom can only be understood through the perceptions of the student. Since learning occurs inside individuals, to monitor learning requires some grasp of how the process is being perceived by the learner. It's a small wonder the capacity for sensitivity or empathy is a major characteristic of good teachers in the findings of many researches. What kind of atmospheres teachers create for the learning process will be determined in large part by their awareness of what goes on in the private worlds of students.

In Chapter 3 I spoke of the "reading behavior backwards" technique for improving empathic understanding. I try to use this technique to become aware of how the world looks to my students, especially how they perceive themselves, how they feel about whatever task they are involved in, and how they see me. These insights invariably provide important clues for improving the atmosphere in my classes. To further help me understand where students are coming from I have employed various devices to open lines of communication with students, a few of these are:

Making classes informal as possible
Operating on a first name basis if comfortable
Taking early opportunities to laugh at myself or express
  chagrin over a personal error
Making it easy as possible to get in touch with me

Responding to student feelings with respect and
   appreciation
Showing concern for student comfort
Encouraging questions and participation
Expressing faith in student capacities and possibilities
Minimizing rules, regulations, and requirements.

Effective Atmospheres Start from Acceptance

Since learning is personal and individual it must start
where students are. People cannot go from where they are
not—only from where they are. Counselors know, for example, that
until an alcoholic can say, "I am an alcoholic," therapy can hardly
get started. Effective teaching, too, must begin with acceptance of
students as they are, where they are, and who they are. The principle is violated, however, in hundreds of ways in our public schools.
It is violated, for example, by age and grade grouping. It is violated
by common requirements for everyone, by teachers who ignore
varying stages of readiness or skill in students, and even by teacher
aspirations for students. Thousands of well meaning teachers, determined that students shall achieve "Excellence," set goals and expectations so high that the message they convey to students is: "You are
failing, reprehensible, or second rate because you are not where I
think you should be."

Failing to accept students where they are, many
teachers eat their hearts out wishing students were better, smarter, or
more committed. Others seek excuses for students who do not
achieve teacher expectations by blaming students, parents, the community, or the administration for requiring teachers to work with students so badly prepared or motivated. Understanding the individual
and personal character of learning has helped me greatly to accept
"the great unwashed public" just as it comes. I try to accept each student as and where the student is, then help each one as far along the
path of personal growth as I can in the time I have with him or her. I
still want the best for students but I find that acceptance frees both

the student and me from the demands of irrelevant expectations to concentrate on the here and now. As a consequence my goals are more realistic and far more comfortable for both of us.

Removing Barriers to Learning

Creating facilitative atmospheres for learning requires thinking in two ways about the matter. First, one must become aware of and remove existing barriers to learning.[4] After that, it is necessary actively to create stimulating and encouraging atmospheres. Even a cursory glance about our public schools will quickly make one aware of innumerable barriers to learning at *every* level of organization and practice. Hindrances to learning may occur in physical settings as, when temperatures are uncomfortable, chairs are bolted to the floor, or lighting is bad. They may also occur for lack of proper equipment, supplies, or inadequate time arrangements. They may be created by the teacher's interactions with students, they may be imposed by administrative demands or curriculum requirements, or they may occur in behaviors, attitudes, habits, or beliefs of students themselves. Whatever the source, the first steps toward creating effective atmospheres require eliminating, neutralizing, or modifying barriers already in place.

As counselor and teacher, over the years I have learned to search for the barriers that keep my students and clients from becoming involved in the teaching or counseling process. I make a practice of asking myself, "What is keeping my students from getting into the act?" "What are the barriers in the way of making this class, this hour, this project an effective learning experience?" Even—"What is it in me that is preventing full student participation?" Having brought to light possible barriers by such questions, I then seek systematically to eliminate them from the learning situations I am trying to create. The technique is especially relevant when working with culturally diverse students. It has sharpened my perceptions about the dynamics of what is going on in my classes and interactions with my students. Often the very process of becoming aware of existing barriers suggests effective modes of action for eliminating

them. Conscious searching for barriers has also helped me see myself more clearly and provided important opportunities to clarify my
personal meanings by subjecting them to confrontation with real situations.

Challenge and Threat

I have found additional clues for the creation of atmospheres conducive to learning in the principles determining threat
and challenge. As we have seen, a major factor in learning is related
to the student's experience of challenge or threat. People feel challenged when they are confronted with problems that interest them
and with which they believe they have a chance of being successful.
They feel threatened when confronted with problems that seem to
them beyond their capacities. These experiences have vital bearing
on the degree to which students are likely to become involved in
learning experiences. Effective atmospheres for learning are likely to
be challenging without being threatening. To produce such atmospheres teachers can find clues to action in any aspect of the dynamics involved. They can concentrate on student interest by trying
to relate information or experience to student need. Or, teachers can
adjust the difficulty of materials to the student's perceived adequacy
so students believe they have a good chance for success. Or,
teachers can concentrate attention on the student's sense of adequacy directly, building student self-concepts to a point where students perceive events as challenging rather than threatening because
they see themselves as more able to cope.

Teachers can also facilitate effective learning atmospheres through the uses they make of themselves while interacting
with students. By the attitudes we express in words or actions, by the
questions we ask, by the encouragement or discouragement we express, by the support we provide, by enthusiasm we show, or by the
acceptance or rejection of student ideas, students are helped or
hindered to explore the meaning of curricula, issues, facts, and
ideas. Research has shown that the essence of good teaching has to
do with the ways in which teachers have learned to use themselves
as instruments in the teaching process. The teacher's self is the pri-

mary instrument with which the teacher must work, and the choices made about how to use that self effectively assists or hinders students in the processes of learnng.

PROVIDING INFORMATION OR EXPERIENCE

The second prime task of the teacher has to do with facilitating student acquisition of new information or experience. This is the aspect of learning with which teachers have traditionally been most proficient. They are knowledgeable people and imparting information is the thing they do best. Teachers are experts at providing students with information through lectures, books, movies, demonstrations, and the like. In modern thinking about learning, however, helping students acquire information is only one step in a process that goes far beyond mere provision of information. Learning must be understood in terms of student experience. Learning is an active process and mere listening, reading, or watching is no guarantee that information is experienced at any significant level.

Experiential Learning

Experiential learning is more student centered than teacher or content centered. It concentrates attention upon what the student is making of information. Experiential approaches to learning call for actively encountering information or events in some fashion and the vigorous participation of students in the learning process may often prove to be more important for student growth than exposure to a given curriculum.

The ways in which good teachers help students experience new information are almost limitless. Many depend on various forms of problem solving specifically arranged by the teacher. They may also arise out of the student's own questions or teachers may simply capitalize on spontaneous problems arising in the course of classroom activities, field trips, laboratory conditions, and the like.

Teachers can also aid experiential learning by suggesting new and more fruitful ways to attack problems. They may do it by establishing attitudes that "it is good to look and fun to try." They may do it by setting examples or by inspiring students to explore new and unfamiliar territory, the very essence of creativity. The extension of student awareness, daring to leave the comfort and security of the familiar to explore uncharted ground, to seek new experience, to encounter new problems, and to seek new answers or expressions, is what education is all about.

The principle of "pacing" has long been a guideline for elementary teachers. It refers to the adjustment of learning situations to the capacities and readiness of students. Other ways in which teachers may facilitate learning and experience have to do with creating bite-sized problems, fitting problems confronted to student readiness and capacity. Often this can be done by breaking larger questions into smaller ones capable of solution at the student's current level of knowledge and skill. It can also be accomplished by helping students acquire the basic skills needed to deal with problems. Teachers can also assist through building up the student's own personal resources provided by positive self-concepts or experiences of success.

Concentrating on Structure

One way of helping students confront information more efficiently is to concentrate attention on the structure of knowledge rather than the accumulation of facts. The curriculum in any subject always includes basic principles that hold facts together and give them meaning. This structure of knowledge is far more important for understanding a subject than the myriad of facts that hang upon it. To help the student explore basic principles however, requires that teachers demonstrate their importance by concentrating on them, for students assume that teachers know what is important and follow their spoken or unspoken directions. Unfortunately, it is easy for teachers to be seduced into concentrating heavily on facts simply because there are so many of them. The curriculum in any subject is usually composed of a multitude of facts and a comparative handful of fundamental principles. This often produces a self-defeating scenario that goes like this: Teachers must meet their classes many times in the course of a year, semester, or quarter, but the number of basic principles in any subject is comparatively few. There are thousands of facts in any content field; consequently, teachers find themselves spending most of class time with their enumeration. Students, on their part, observing the teacher's concentration upon details, assume they must be important. Accordingly, they carefully fill their notebooks with as many facts as possible and miss or bury the basic principles. The matter may be further complicated by the use of objective testing for student evaluation. To spread students out on the good old normal curve requires large numbers of test items. Since there are only a few basic principles but hundreds of facts, the tests tend to concentrate on details. This further corroborates student belief that it is the details that must be mastered. The net result finds both teachers and students concentrating on details rather than the structure or meaning of information. Teachers truly concerned about exploring the meaning of concepts and ideas need to be on guard against falling into such traps.

Preoccupation with neatness, punctuation, facts, forms, grades, conformity, minutiae, and "being right" inevitably conveys those priorities to students who "get the message" and organize their efforts accordingly. Teachers who value student beliefs, opinions, attitudes, values, personal meanings, and capacity to think about ideas have a different set of priorities and deliver different messages. To facilitate the exploration of personal meaning I try to demonstrate in my teaching that I value meanings more than right answers, student personal experience more than reporting or regurgitating information, and creativity and individuality more than conformity.

Current pressures for educational accountability translated into demands for behavioral objectives or competencies defined in narrow, specific terms also makes teacher attention to structure and meaning more difficult. It concentrates action on minute behavior rather than comprehensive understanding. Students with knowledge of facts but no grasp of structure may be able to pass an objective test today but this is no guarantee they can solve tomorrow's problems calling for deeper understanding. I try to resist such fragmentation of learning and concentrate on structure in whatever subject I may be teaching. I find that students who understand structure and principles can find relevant facts when they are needed, and their performance in whatever evaluative technique I use does not suffer from such emphases.

AIDING DISCOVERY OF MEANING

Finally, teachers can facilitate learning by actively assisting the student's personal exploration of meaning. I believe this is, at once, the most crucial and the most neglected aspect of teaching. The historical role of teachers has been primarily that of information provider. Only recently have we come to understand the significance of experiential learning and many teachers have few skills for facilitating the personal discovery of meaning in their students. Since people only do what seems to them important, the first step in learning to facilitate student discovery of personal meaning is teacher belief that it is important. If teachers do not believe so, it will almost certainly not occur in any significant amounts. Once intelligent teachers grasp the vital importance of this aspect of learning, they can be counted upon to find hundreds of ingenious ways of bringing it about.

Teaching understood as the expert imparting knowledge to the neophyte has produced schools and classrooms almost exclusively focusing upon some form of lecturing, demonstrating, questioning, or examining as primary vehicles by which learning is brought about. This relationship between teacher and student is similar to that between the doctor and patient. The doctor is the expert, the one who knows. He or she makes a diagnosis, decides what is necessary, and tells the patient what the score is and what the patient must do. The doctor is the boss, the patient is the passive recipient of the doctor's knowledge. Such a model for teaching may be useful for the exposure to information or experience aspect of learning. It does very little to forward the second half of the learning problem, the personal discovery of meaning. For that aspect of the problem it is the student who knows and the teacher who does not. The personal discovery of meaning goes on inside the student. That calls for teachers who are helpers, facilitators, assisters, and guides, who are able to involve students deeply in learning processes, and who are skillful in stimulating and encouraging students in the personal discovery of meaning. This is not to say there is no place for lecture-demonstration techniques in teaching. Such time honored practices are, of course, still useful for the new information or experience aspect of learning, but hardly enough to guarantee student discovery of meaning. Truly effective teaching calls for teachers equipped to deal with *both* phases of the learning process.

The Value of Discussion

The discovery of personal meaning is an active process. Among the most effective means for helping students explore and discover new meaning, I find, is participation in group activities, especially those in which students feel safe enough to reveal themselves and get involved with one or more others.[5] This is the way most of us learn our most valuable concepts for living. As ideas are expressed by others, we are confronted with new concepts for digestion. As ideas are bounced around in a group—especially as we introduce ourselves into the act by thinking, expressing, questioning, proposing, agreeing, and rejecting ideas—our own meanings become changed, modified, supported, or rejected. Through such experiences, little by little we fit ideas into place in the larger gestalt of our personal belief systems.

Some people regard discussion groups as a waste of time. One can sometimes hear them complaining, "Discussion groups only compound your confusion," "They just pool your ignorance," or "How do you know when you get the right answer?" Some people are very uncomfortable in discussion groups. They would prefer having someone settle matters by making decisions or telling everyone the "right" answers. As we have already seen many of our most important learnings have nothing to do with new information. They come about as a consequence of deeper and deeper exploration of the personal meaning of ideas we already have.

Group interaction is one of the most valuable techniques available to us for achieving those ends.

One needs but to think about some of his or her most important learnings to recognize how significant groups have been for learning. Most of our truly significant learning experiences came about in interactions with one or more other persons. Very few sprang into being solely from ourselves. Even those which did seem to spring into clear awareness when we were alone probably came into figure as an outgrowth of prior experiences with others. In group settings one has the opportunity to bring attitudes, feelings, and beliefs to light; to subject them to the test of interaction with others; to clarify concepts; and to discover their values and fit them into a more congruent personal belief system.

Groups may be formed for all kinds of purposes depending on the intent of the leader and the group members. In the past twenty to thirty years we have seen a tremendous interest in various kinds of therapy or awareness groups devised to help group members explore themselves and their relationships with the world about them, to increase awareness, to expand consciousness, sensitivity, and the like. Treatment or therapy groups have sometimes been adapted for educational settings, but groups of most value to students, I think, are the kind I have described as learning or discussion groups.

Learning or Discussion Groups

It is easy for a group of people to engage in talk, but this does not mean that there exists a group discussion. A group discussion is not a debate. Neither is it a bull session. The purpose of a debate is to convince other people of the rightness of one's own position. "Convincing" may even proceed without any real regard for accuracy, but only with a desire to win the argument irrespective of the merits of the position. A bull session, on the other hand, is a pleasant sort of pastime in which one seeks to regale others by descriptions or stories of things one knows or of personal experiences. Bull sessions are a kind of friendly game of "one-upmanship" in which one person tells a story and the next seeks to top it with still another. Good group discussions are neither of these. The purpose of group discussion is neither to win an argument nor to amuse one's self. Its purpose is to explore and discover personal meanings.

There are two kinds of group discussions in general use in teaching. One is the "Decision Group" in which the primary purpose is to arrive at a consensus or decision on some matter. Almost everyone is familiar with such groups and has participated in them at one time or another. Decision groups can be very helpful in bringing about an agreement on a plan of action. Unfortunately, they may also interfere with the freedom of the individual to explore and move in directions unique to personal needs, for decision groups have the unhappy effect of coercing their members to arrive at the approved solutions.

A second type of discussion group is the "Exploratory" or "Learning" Group. In these sessions the purpose is not to arrive at decisions, but to help each member explore ideas and discover meanings through interaction with other people. It is intriguing to watch the development of a good group. One can almost measure the degree of significance in the level of talk. Groups generally begin with what I call "finger tip" or "arm's length" talk, mostly description with little personal involvement. Much of our everyday talk is of that sort as we seek to convey ideas to other people. It usually proceeds with such expressions as "I saw," "I said," "He told me," "There was," etc. As groups warm up, get acquainted, begin to trust the process, conversation comes increasingly closer to self. At first this is tentative with such expressions as "It seems to me," "I'm not sure about this but," "Sometimes I wonder if," "What do you think about?" As people become more involved one can detect more personal involvement: "I think," "I believe," "I wish." After that discussion becomes more personal and daring: "I think and here's why," "I like, dislike." And, if a group feels very safe with each other deeply personal meanings may be shared: "I'm afraid," "I'm angry about" or "I love."

Group discussion does not seek to convince; rather, it deals with matters unsolved and seeks to help each member find meanings not existing before. It is often tentative, even halting, in its progress, for it deals not with certainty but with search. It is an exploration of feelings, beliefs, doubts, fears, and concerns. Good groups take time to form and it is only as the members of a group discover each other as warm friendly people that good group discussion can come about. To facilitate development of such atmospheres, I sometimes find it helps to provide my students with the following hints:

1   For good thinking there must be a sense of relaxation. Discussion should always be leisurely, not desultory or wandering, but also not hastened or tense. It is more important to think slowly and thoroughly than to cover any prearranged amount of material.

2   Although we hope that all members of our groups will feel free to contribute to the discussion and will want to share their thinking with others, we also recognize that for some people this is a difficult and trying thing to do. No one is under compulsion to speak. Participation is not measured by words spoken; a silent person may be participating more than more verbal colleagues.

3   The purpose of group discussion is the discovery of personal meaning. This calls for kicking ideas around, testing them, trying them on for size, examining, comparing, thinking about and talking about ideas until they fit the particular needs of each person. This is best accomplished when group members are willing to express their own thinking, beliefs, and feelings freely on the one hand and to listen receptively and sympathetically to other people's ideas.

4   Sometimes there may be periods of silence. These need not cause concern. They are normal happenings that occur at points when a group is thinking deeply, is in process of shifting gears, or has exhausted a particular question.

5   Discussion proceeds best in an atmosphere of warmth and friendliness. Nothing causes people to clam up quicker than being threatened, ridiculed, or humiliated. An atmosphere of acceptance and honest seeking for understanding is most conducive to good group operation. The more quickly you can get to know and appreciate your fellow group members as individual people, the more quickly your group will begin to pay dividends in growth and development of its members.

Discovering Meaning Takes Time

Learning understood as the exploration and discovery of personal meaning is a time-consuming process. It takes time to explore and discover new meanings. What is more, the more important the learning for the student, the longer the process will probably take. It takes but a moment to read or hear an idea. To comprehend its meaning and ramifications and make it part of one's self is a very different matter. Failure to fully appreciate the time-consuming aspect of real learning results in great frustration for many teachers. Under pressure to "cover the subject," "prepare for the test," "meet the deadline," or "achieve the stated objectives," many a teacher has frustrated and interfered with the very process of learning he or she sought to encourage. Like providing children food, preparing it and offering it can be greatly speeded up; digesting it can only be done by the child at his or her own rate of speed. I find facilitating personal meaning demands great patience. There are strict limits to how much learning processes can be hurried and the very desire of teachers for student achievement can cause students to push so hard as to impede or destory the learning process itself.

Concomitant Learning

In addition to the easily recognized aspects of learning going on at any moment, effective teaching requires awareness of the side effects of teaching as well. Because learning occurs inside people, teachers cannot always be cognizant of just what is occurring in the perceptual fields of students. Often the meanings students derive may be far afield from those intended by the teacher. These side effects often show up in their wildest or hilarious form in written work or on examinations. Every teacher has groaned or giggled at student "boners," those weird distortions learners sometimes acquire despite the teacher's most valiant efforts at clear presentations. "Boners" represent simple distortions of subject matter, and, however frustrating to teachers, are seldom serious in their effects upon student lives. Other forms of concomitant learning have to do with personal meanings having little or nothing to do with subject matter.

Student perceptions are not limited to events teachers intend. Students perceive the entire situations in which they are involved. So, in a classroom they may be perceiving and learning about themselves, about their teachers, about other students, or any of thousands of other possibilities. What is more, these side effects or concomitants may often be far more significant than those learnings on which the teacher is concentrating. That a student is learning he is stupid, that her teacher is a phoney, that other students think he or she is a clown, or that speaking before a class is humiliating may be far more important personal learnings than the curriculum planned for that day. Effective teaching requires the clearest possible understanding of what is going on in the student's perceptual world. No one, of course, can ever know precisely how another person is thinking, perceiving, or believing; but the more teachers can be aware of what students are *really* learning, the more they will be able to construct effective strategies for teaching.

The last thirty or forty years have seen a development of many different approaches to teaching for more effective personal learning. These may be found under such headings as workshop learning, democratic classrooms, self-directed learning, discovery learning, humanistic teaching, contract learning, inquiry, schools without failure, even progressive education. By whatever name, each advocates ways of teaching designed to move beyond the traditional lecture-demonstration techniques to encourage and assist students in the personal discovery of meaning. Though I have not totally committed myself to any one of these new and promising approaches to teaching, I have borrowed liberally from many of them to implement my own beliefs about effective teaching and learning. In the endnotes for this chapter I have included a sample bibliography which may serve as an introduction to some of the most promising techniques for advancing personal discovery of learning.[6]

SOME IMPLICATIONS OF NEED FOR TEACHING

A frequent complaint of grown ups about modern youth is that they are "so apathetic." Apathy is treated as though it were a cause of not learning. Actually it is not a cause of anything. Apathy is a result. It is the reaction people have when confronted with problems irrelevant to their personal needs or which seem too much for them to handle successfully. A common complaint of many young people these days is that their schools are "irrelevant." This is another way of saying that schools do not seem to them to fill their personal needs. Few of us get very excited about matters that seem irrelevant.

Despite the crucial character of need for learning, the principle is widely ignored in most teaching practice. The curricula of schools are determined mostly by adults who decide what students will need to know in the years ahead. Whether students perceive such need is rarely examined and little or no energy is expended to help students develop needs to know.

A complicating factor in the effect of need on learning is the fact that people are primarily motivated by immediate needs. Few of us are much stimulated to action by far-off or seemingly unattainable goals unless they can be broken down to more immediate subgoals capable of providing some current satisfaction. The need of the school is to prepare young people for the future; student needs exist in the present. This dilemma is responsible for many of the problems of education. Here and there, teachers, and occasionally whole schools, have made extensive efforts to find ways of fulfilling students' immediate needs without sacrificing the long-term objectives of schooling. Generally, however, most schools and teachers have given little more than lip service to the significance of need in learning. The principle cannot be set aside however. It will not go away. It is vital to learning and failure to understand and apply it to teaching will continue to frustrate one's very best efforts.[7]

Harnessing the Motivation of Need

Understanding the importance and significance of student need does not require me to let students do anything they please. That would be an abdication of my responsibility as a teacher. Many student needs, of course, cannot be immediately satisfied by schools or teachers. Moment to moment needs may also be so tangential as to have little or no educational significance. Still others may be downright counterproductive or destructive to effective learning. Being concerned about student needs does not require either that I forgo the goals society has for its schools. Quite the contrary. Understanding student needs makes it possible for me to utilize the enormous power of personal needs to help students achieve educational objectives. As I learn to work *with* them, rather than *against* them, I harness their motivating force to the eventual fulfillment of both the students' and society's needs. My task as a teacher is not simply to fulfill student needs. The genius of good teaching lies in helping students fulfill their current needs, then, helping them discover needs they never knew they had. Adapting my teaching to the needs of my students is not mere indulgence of student whims. Quite the contrary. It is acceptance of the fact that students have personal needs and the utilization of those needs to facilitate the processes of learning. I am using a powerful tool to advance the learning process.

The notion of improving learning by adapting teaching to the needs and purposes of students is by no means new. Thousands of teachers employ the principle of relating learning to student need in classes everyday. There is also much evidence to demonstrate that schools, classes, or teachers that help students fulfill their basic needs pay off much better in student motivation and achievement. I have been trying to find ways of relating my teaching to student needs for a very long time and it pays big dividends not only in student accomplishment but also in furthering my own growth and development.

School curricula are usually established in some sort of orderly sequence determined by the logical flow of subject matter. This neat organization, however appropriate from a subject matter view point, may not be efficient for the encouragement of learning. Students rarely learn in orderly logical ways. They acquire information in response to immediate needs, personal experiences, or problems confronted. Such "disorderly" approaches to subject matter can sometimes drive teachers crazy. People who have spent their professional lives in a particular content area develop deep appreciation for the order and symmetry of their subject. They love its logical order, the flow of its organization from simple basics to complex patterns and functions. Unhappily, students do not learn so. They want to know things quite out of sequence or in response to personal need unknown to teachers. This can be a frustrating and painful experience for teachers who love their subject and long for students to share their appreciation of its majesty and discipline. It is easy to forget that people do not learn in orderly ways, that order is imposed upon content only after the content is grasped.

I have discovered that if I find ways of adjusting content of whatever I'm teaching to the needs of students they will want to know about 70 percent of what I had planned to present. So, 30 percent of what I had planned to present they do not cover. On the other hand, there is another 30 percent that they want to know about that I never thought to include when making my plans. It is that 30 percent, I find, that keeps me alive and interested year after year. I grow, too, as students see relationships that never occurred to me, ask questions I never thought of, or want to explore in directions I never perceived.

Expanding Need

The implications of all this for my teaching is that:

1   I must do what I can to help students fulfill or deal wiith those needs interfering with involvement in learning

processes. Some of these, like fatigue or comfort or student fears about what I may think about them, are well within my control. Some I can sometimes influence by seeking the assistance of parents, administrators, or colleagues, or through my own involvement in needed educational reforms. And some are so totally outside my sphere of influence that I can do little more than be appreciative or supportive of the students' feelings of frustration, anger, or deprivation.

2   Second, I can try to find ways of utilizing the student's current needs as motivation for learning. I can, for instance, try to relate the subject matter we are covering to the student's own needs. I can keep in touch with the current world of students and attempt to plan explorations of subject matter in ways related to their current problems. One of the nice things about teaching psychology is that it has such broad applications to everyday life and so much of its subject matter has immediate relevance to the problems students confront both in and out of school.

3   Finally, if I am to properly carry out my role as teacher I must assist students to expand their current needs to perceive new ones the student may never have seen before.[8] I can create new needs to know. This is the broadening, expanding, inspirational, creative aspect of teaching. Without this phase, teaching is little more than maintaining the status quo.

There are many ways to create needs to know. Some elementary teachers, for example, try to help students see a need for learning by setting up a store in the classroom. This provides children with opportunities to see a need for arithmetic because they have to make change, for writing because they need to make a sign, for reading because they need to know what are in the boxes and cans on the shelves. In upper grades, and in higher education most teachers spend little or no effort in trying to relate learning to student needs. Teachers are likely to assume that students have a need to know whatever the teacher is covering, or if they don't they should. Many disillusioned ones, alas, assume students do not have a need and little can be done about it and so plug away at trying to teach them anyhow.

By all odds the most frequently encountered attempts to relate student needs to learning is to provide some artificial reason for learning in the form of rewards or punishments unrelated to the subject matter being explored. Grades or marking systems are the most obvious of the formal devices employed to create artificial reasons for learning. They are also woefully inadequate as motivators for most students.

In my own experience, needs arising from the students' own interactions with the world are likely to be most effective in stimulating learning. Needs arising from direct contact with people and events are immediate, spontaneous, and likely to be far more pressing than artificial ones. A good example of the application of this principle can be seen in teachers' colleges which have changed their thinking about "practice teaching." Formerly, practice teaching typically came at the end of the training program. The idea was that teachers in training learned how to teach from their professors at the college then went out to "practice" in the schools. More recently, teachers' colleges have come to value field experience for its contributions in helping students in training to discover needs to know, to understand what the problems are. Accordingly, many schools are now requiring field experience throughout the period of training rather than just at the end. There is probably nothing like actual participation in the field one hopes to work in for opening one's eyes or confronting one with problems needing solution. Field experience has additional motivational value in the fact that whatever is learned has almost immediate application, provides opportunity to observe results and the glow of satisfaction which comes from being able successfully to put one's learning to a practical test.

Another invaluable source of need discovery is participation in groups. Despite generations of teachers' admonitions to students to "work by yourself," students continue to seek interaction with peers because they know it works better—and besides, it is more fun. Learning is a highly social process and most of us develop our most pressing needs to know as a consequence of social interactions. Development of needs to know in groups is especially likely to be fruitful when groups are confronted with common problems, are involved in cooperative activities or when members feel responsible, not only for themselves, but for the rest of the group as well.

CHAPTER 6

About Goals and Purposes

People behave in terms of their purposes, and teachers are no exception. All sorts of purposes determine teacher behavior: some broad and general, like beliefs about the goals of education; some much more specific, like beliefs about the proper objectives for the teacher's special subject; or even fleeting, moment to moment purposes, like "what response I want from Helen in answer to my question." The very nature of the teaching profession keeps teachers immersed in purposes every moment. In addition to the goals and purposes of the community that owns the schools, and the expectations of administrators, parents, and supervisors, there are the needs and aspirations of the students, to say nothing of the teacher's own goals and purposes to contend with. All need to be brought into sufficient harmony so that the teacher's professional goals have a fighting chance to be achieved.

What people believe about the goals and purposes of education makes a great deal of difference in the choices they make and the ways they behave. Some people believe the purpose of our public schools, for example, is to produce the leaders of the future. Others think the maximum development of every child is the proper goal. Which of these beliefs one holds is likely to produce quite different answers to questions about school financing, programs for the handicapped or "slower" children, matters of discipline, attitudes toward drop outs and gifted children, and dozens of other questions. Beliefs about school aims and objectives also provide important guidelines for teacher behavior and must therefore be important aspects of a personal theory of teaching. The specific aims of teachers, of course, are too personal and complex to deal with in a book like this. We can, however, explore more general goals about what society wants from its schools, what teachers want for students, and the relationships of these to each other. Accordingly, in the remainder of this chapter I have tried to set down my beliefs about these matters for what they may be worth to others thinking about their personal approach to teaching.

SOCIETY'S NEEDS

A major purpose for the founding of our first public schools in America was to assure that young people would grow up able to read the Bible. Over the years, this narrow, original purpose has been greatly expanded to encompass the development of responsible, productive citizens. No modern society can afford to let its young people grow up without education. For generations schools have attempted to teach youth the basic tools for learning and whatever else the society considered most essential for the induction of youth into the larger culture. An educational system is one of society's ways of perpetuating its existence.

Some people have suggested that public schools ought to indoctrinate youth in such fashion that a new and better social order might come into being. Such exalted dreams for education seem highly unlikely to be achieved however, for no society is likely to tolerate for very long an attempt by one of its own institutions to overthrow it. Schools are designed to perpetuate society. While some deviation from this goal is occasionally permitted, public schools that depart very far from society's fundamental purposes are not likely to be supported or indulged for very long. This fact may seem disappointing to persons deeply concerned about failures of our current society to move more rapidly toward lofty human objectives. Nevertheless, as we shall see further on, our public schools can be significant agents of social change and yet remain acceptable to the society supporting them.

Seven Basic Objectives

Society's primary purpose in establishing public schools is the production of intelligent, responsible citizens. While the specific goals through which that aim is to be achieved may vary from generation to generation, society supports its schools primarily to prepare youth to assume the duties of full-fledged membership. Within that broad objective Americans have stated and restated their goals for education for 250 years. A comprehensive review of these from the very beginning right down to those produced at the last White House Conference boils down to seven basic objectives which parents, scholars, educators, and public officials have advocated repeatedly down the years. They are:

1 Command of fundamental processes and skills for learning
2 Preparation for worthy home membership
3 Civic education for responsible citizenship
4 Physical and mental health
5 Basic skills for taking one's place in the world of work
6 Effective use of leisure time
7 Education for moral and ethical character.

Additional Purposes Society Seeks for Its Schools

In addition to the general purpose of preparing intelligent and responsible citizens, communities use their schools for more immediate purposes—sometimes generally, sometimes on a purely local basis. In recent years, for example, we have seen the public schools used as a vehicle to correct the social ills of segregation. Some states also seek to indoctrinate democratic ideals by requiring students to take a course in "Democracy vs. Communism."

In some communities, schools are highly valued as an agency for keeping students off the streets or out of the job market. In others, schools are expected to exert positive influences on youth through required courses in alcohol or drug abuse, driver or sex education, and the like. And, of course, high on the list of community expectations from its public schools in many places may be public entertainment and upholding of community honor through competitive sport programs.

Our educational system, of course, cannot accept complete responsibility for all these objectives. Crucial influences are exerted on young people by many other forces in our society. That fact does not permit us to wash our hands of the matter, however. Quite the contrary. We have to contribute whatever schools can to what the public wants for its youth. Clear understandings of society's goals and objectives for its schools must always be important ingredients in the formulation of an effective teacher's personal system of beliefs.

ACTUALIZATION OR FULFILLMENT AS THE GOAL OF SOCIETY AND INDIVIDUALS

People band together to form groups in order to fulfill individual needs. By identifying with other persons seeking need satisfaction in ways similar to their own, people are able to achieve greater satisfaction than they would be able to by themselves. This is the fundamental reason for the formation of groups, whether we are talking about two people joining to make a family, or larger numbers getting together to form a club, school, industry, or nation. Once identified with a group, an individual thereafter tends to adopt and defend the standards and behavior of the group he or she has joined. Groups will continue to exist only so long as they serve reasonably well to satisfy the needs of their members. People tend to withdraw from groups whose approval they are unable to win or which no longer satisfy their needs. This intimate relationship of individuals with their groups or societies means that the fundamental purposes of healthy societies and individuals are essentially the same—the personal fulfillment of members.

If the basic goal of society and its individuals is personal fulfillment, we need then to ask what is the nature of such fulfillment? As we have seen in Chapter 2 the primary need of all human beings is to move toward health or self-actualization. For many years health was regarded primarily as a matter of being "well" or "not sick" in physical terms. In psychological terms it was regarded as being "nondeviant," a question of a person's position on the good old normal curve into which human traits seem to fall. Most people on such a curve cluster about the middle of the distribution with the "maladjusted" at each end. This conception of health has never been very satisfying for persons in the field of counseling and teaching, for it fails to provide a reasonable goal for desirable growth. Who, after all, wants to be average?

More recently, psychologists, like workers in other professions, have been looking at the question of fulfillment in terms of ultimate goals. In medicine, for example, investigators have been exploring what it means to be superbly healthy. They speak of the concept of "high-level wellness." In psychology, workers have been exploring the nature of self-actualization—what it means to be self-fulfilling in the highest possible sense. Such thinking is tremendously important for the helping professions, for whatever we decide truly healthy, self-fulfilling persons are like, must also become the primary goal of the helping professions including education. That is the theme of the 1962 ASCD Yearbook, *Perceiving Behaving Becoming: A New Focus for Education.*[1] This classic begins with statements from four scholars about the nature of self-actualization. The remainder of the book is devoted to exploring what those ideas mean for educational thought and practice. Despite the date of its publication, the book is as pertinent today as it was in 1962.

What Is Self-Actualization or Fulfillment?

There are two ways in which we may look at the question of self-actualization. One way is to explore the matter from an external frame of reference; that is, from the point of view of an outsider. One asks, "What are the characteristic traits of highly self-actualizing persons?" This is the approach taken by such observers as Carl Rogers and Abraham Maslow.[2] From an examination of their writings we find such characteristics listed as: openness to experience; living in a more existential fashion; having an increasing trust in the organism; acceptance of self, others, and nature; spontaneity; problem centering; autonomy; independence of culture and environment; freshness of appreciation; clear discrimination between means and ends; an unhostile sense of humor; creativeness; and resistence to enculturation.

Listing the traits of self-actualizing persons is helpful, but it is essentially descriptive. It tells us what such persons are like yet provides us little help in understanding the dynamics of how they got that way. Knowing that self-actualizing persons are creative, trust their organisms, or have freshness of appreciation or an unhostile sense of humor, for example, still leaves us with the problem of how to facilitate the development of such traits. Trait descriptions, however accurate, do not themselves provide us with guidelines to action. We need to understand self-actualizing persons in dynamic terms that tell us how such traits come into being.

My own preference is to seek understanding of self-actualization from an internal frame of reference, through understanding of the perceptual organization of self-actualizing persons. This approach attempts to explore how such persons see themselves and the world in which they are operating. It also seems to me to provide more immediate and useful clues for ways of helping persons achieve more satisfying levels of self-fulfillment. Examined in this way, self-actualizing persons seem possessed of four major characteristics:

1   They are knowledgeable people.
2   They see themselves in positive ways.
3   The are open to experience.
4   They have deep feelings of identification with others.[3]

Knowledge and Self-Actualization

It would be pretty difficult in our complex world to be stupid and achieve much self-actualization. To function even passably in our society requires considerable knowledge. To function extremely well requires a great deal more. Self-actualizing persons are well informed about themselves and the world in which they operate. As a consequence, they are able to behave more intelligently, appropriately, and successfully than less well-informed persons. A major function of education has always been to achieve this end. Schools have always sought to promote student growth and development through helping them become better informed and so more able to cope effectively with life.

Though being informed is a major characteristic of self-actualization, there is, as yet, no research to demonstrate that such knowledge is necessarily academic. Many "intellectuals," though well informed academically, still operate in non-self actualizing ways. One may also find highly self-actualizing persons with comparatively little academic knowledge who are highly knowledgeable about the world and the people they live and work with. I have known a self-actualizing farmer and a fisherman with little formal education, for example. I have also had the pleasure of observing several self-actualized children who have not even started school.

Positive Views of Self

Highly self-actualizing persons are generally characterized by positive views of self. They see themselves as liked, wanted, acceptable, able, and as persons of dignity and integrity. Such feelings provide great advantage for interacting successfully with the world. Seeing one's self in positive ways provides a secure and stable base from which to launch excursions into the world. Feeling basically secure, such people can afford to take risks; hence, they are more likely to be creative and innovative. Problems of living can be approached with confidence and satisfaction; therefore, those individuals are more likely to be successful. Feeling good about self, one can deal with life straight forwardly and authentically instead of fearfully and tentatively. Other people are very likely to respond in positive ways to persons who act with assurance. Self-actualizing persons are strong personalities and other people are often greatly attracted to them.[4]

This circular effect is characteristic of self-actualization—the strong get stronger and the weak get weaker. Persons who behave with deep assurance convey assurance in their behavior. Such assurance, in turn, creates trust in those they work with and the likelihood of more successful action. Successful outcomes in turn only corroborate the already positive views of self possessed by self-actualizing persons.

The reverse is true for persons who see themselves in negative ways. Approaching life problems tentatively and timidly, their efforts are likely to be self-defeating and the feedback they get from consequent failure only serves to prove the accuracy of their already negative views of self. Just as positive views of self are characteristic of highly self-actualizing people, low self-esteem is a frequently found dynamic in the personalities of unsuccessful, unhappy, and mentally ill persons. Such people often see themselves as unliked, unwanted, unacceptable, unable, etc. They upset their parents, cause trouble in school or community, and grow up to fill our jails and mental hospitals.

A positive self-concept is a tremendous personal resource. Many of the characteristics of self-actualizing persons listed by Maslow and Rogers are either a direct outgrowth or strongly influenced by positive views of self. Such traits as comfortable relationships with reality, acceptance of self, autonomy, independence of culture and environment, unhostile sense of humor, living in a more existential fashion, and increasing trust in the organism, for example, are likely to be behavioral expressions of strong self-concepts. In the life-long struggle of human beings for health and personal fulfillment, a positive view of self provides an enormous advantage which self-actualizing persons have achieved in high degree. A major goal for teaching must be the production of positive selves in the largest possible numbers of students. The achievement of such a goal will not only contribute to the health and fulfillment of students; it will contribute as well to the health and fulfillment of society.

Openness to Experience

Self-actualizing persons have a high degree of ability to confront the world and enter into effective and satisfying transactions with it. They seem far more able than most people to confront the world accurately, realistically, and with a minimum of distortion. To enter into effective dialogue with the world requires being willing and able to confront it as it is. Psychologists call this "acceptance," but it should not be confused with resignation. Self-actualizing persons can confront unpleasant aspects of themselves and the world straightforwardly. They are able to say, "Yes, it is true. Sometimes I am impatient, unfair . . .," or whatever. They are not resigned to such conditions however. They do the best they can to deal with such events. A major factor contributing to their ability to do this is the possession of positive views of self. High levels of self-esteem characteristic of self-actualizing people make it easy for them to operate with openness to experience as well.

Persons confronted with data or experiences different from or antagonistic to their belief systems often react by trying to deny the events before them. They may ignore the experience, behave as though it did not exist, or claim "it isn't so." Another way of living with unpleasant ideas is to distort them in some fashion to make them fit what the person would like to believe. In this fashion it is possible to avoid an unpleasant situation and come out "smelling like a rose." So, people may cheat an insurance company with the rationalization that "big companies like that expect it" or avoid the responsibility of helping the poor and unfortunate with a statement like, "They like it that way." A much healthier way to deal with noxious perceptions is to confront them squarely and deal with them in whatever manner is truly appropriate. That approach is far more characteristic of self-actualizing persons.

Openness to experience characteristic of self-actualizing persons is also likely to result in more intelligent behavior. Greater openness to experience means persons have more data from which to make choices. More data, in turn, is likely to result in more effective and appropriate choices of behavior. More successful behavior, in its turn, provides the behaver with greater success experience, more positive views of self, and contributes to further self-actualization. So, "the rich get richer and the poor get poorer." Helping students develop openness to experience is one of the things that education is all about. It is the task of schools and teachers to widen the horizons of students, to open their eyes and ears, and to learn to confront themselves and the world with courage and skill.

Identification and Self-Actualization

Self-actualizing persons are characterized by deep feelings of identification with other people. They have a feeling of continuity with all humanity: a sense of oneness in the human condition. Such feelings about other people make it possible for self-actualizing persons to enter into relationships much more openly and deeply. They are able to trust other people and, since all of us tend to react in terms of expectancies, other people generally respond to self-actualizing persons in far more positive ways.

Feelings of belonging are immensely facilitating to almost any human activity. Feelings of alienation, on the other hand, inhibit people's involvement and effective functioning. The deep feelings of identification and caring possessed by self-actualizing persons provide enormous advantages in responding to life. They are not crippled in action by doubts and fears of rejection. Quite the contrary. They enter situations expecting to be accepted and cared about. In addition, their deep feelings of oneness in the human condition make most self-actualizing persons deeply compassionate people. As a consequence, they are likely to be attractive persons to most other people whom they encounter.

We have already seen in our discussion of a theory of learning (Chapter 4) how feelings of belonging affect the process of learning. Those facts alone would make identification and caring vital goals for education. The importance of identification and caring for the production of self-actualization makes them equally important educational goals for the personal fulfillment of students and maximum contribution to the welfare of society.

Students, like everyone else, are forever seeking self-actualization. The way they do this, however, is almost never in such nice, neat goals as those outlined in the previous discussion of self-actualization. The expressions of student search for self-actualization from day to day and moment to moment are likely to be couched in more specific, immediate terms. Whatever the purpose, to get a date, learn mathematics, win a game, avoid humiliation, or a million others, purposes can all be understood as ways to achieve self-actualization when seen through the eyes of the person involved. As we have seen, people can, will, must move toward health and fulfillment if the way seems open to them; students too.

CAN SOCIETAL AND INDIVIDUAL
PURPOSES BE RECONCILED?

Can the goals of society for its schools be reconciled with student needs for self-actualization? At first glance, the purposes of these two populations seem quite diverse. One is social, the other individual; the goal of society is remote, the purposes of students are immediate; one concentrates on desirable behavior, the other on feelings of personal fulfillment. Is it possible these differing purposes can be achieved simultaneously? The answer for me is, yes, but the task is neither simple nor easy.

A major characteristic of modern society is its ever increasing complexity and interdependence. People in today's highly technological societies are utterly dependent upon one another for even the simplest personal satisfactions. Persons in tune with their societies are very likely to find their own needs amply fulfilled. Persons alienated from society, on the other hand, are likely to find their deepest personal needs frustrated and denied.

The humanistic psychology concept of the individual seeking personal ends while simultaneously filling the needs of a group has been called "synergy."[5] Self-actualizing persons characteristically have highly synergic relationships with their societies. A major characteristic of such healthy persons, it will be recalled, is the feeling of identification or oneness with large numbers of humanity. Persons with deep feelings of identification with other human beings cannot harm or destroy their fellows. To do so would be to harm or destroy themselves. In fact, the concept of selfishness disappears as a human dynamic in the very degree to which feelings of identification and self-actualization are realized. When persons feel one with all humankind, then what they do for themselves, they do for others; and what they do for others, they do for themselves as well. Selfishness is thus a characteristic of narrow conceptions of self in persons essentially alienated from other people. Synergic relationships between individuals and their societies can be achieved over a sufficient period of time in the degree to which persons are helped to achieve self-fulfillment. They probably cannot be brought into being by force and coercion or preoccupation with immediate goals by teachers and students.

The more self-actualizing the person, the greater the synergic relationship between the individual and society. Because the relationship of the individual and society is so crucial and because self-actualizing persons have deep feelings of identification with their fellows, the more people achieve personal fulfillment the more likely they are to contribute to the fulfillment of their societies as well. Thus schools that successfully help young people achieve self-actualization at the same time contribute maximally to the societies they represent. By the same token, they also contribute to changing or improving the society which supports them.

Self-actualizing persons are strong, dynamic people. They are also intelligent, knowledgeable, open to experience, and deeply identified with their fellows. These are the very characteristics most likely to produce effective changes in any society. Because self-actualizing persons are successful human beings, they are likely to be admired by others who recognize their strength and so they are pushed or drift into positions of formal or informal leadership. Being open to experience, they are more likely to be creative and innovative and so more likely to be productive or supportive of societal improvements. Their deep feelings of identification also make them compassionate, caring champions of human rights and welfare. They are intelligent, trustworthy, responsible persons—the very kind we need to perceive the need for change and operate effectively in bringing it about.

Healthy students in touch with the realities of their communities will learn to live effectively in them: agreeing, compromising, rejecting the community's inclinations; quietly seeking reform; or actively working to change community directions in full awareness of community responses. Schools and teachers do not need to bewail their inability to change society in some preconceived image. Schools can change their societies over a period of time in the degree to which they are successful in producing self-actualizing human beings. Self-actualizing persons can be counted upon to change the world in the years to come—and probably more effectively from that vantage point than ways we might dream up today. Teachers who contribute to the production of such citizens can count themselves among the most important and effective agents of social change.

SOME IMPLICATIONS FOR PRACTICE

Understanding the purposes of education and society in these terms helps me think about educational problems. It provides important guidelines for both strategy and tactics, for long-range planning, for moment to moment choices and decisions in the classroom, for counseling students or parents, in interacting with administrators and supervisors, and even in conversations in the teachers' lounge. It helps me keep perspective in the selection of goals, materials, and methods of instruction. It is especially useful in times of crisis. When pressures are mounting it helps to keep me on track and prevents me from being unduly influenced by minor issues or irrelevant tangents. Most important, it helps keep me oriented to what is truly important and so to make decisions and choices on more solid bases.

If the relationship between individual need and the needs of society is as close as suggested by the theoretical position discussed, then, it would appear that if we can help students fulfill their personal needs, they will be more likely in the long run to fulfill the needs of society too. Many people have doubts about that. They begin from a belief that students are essentially untrustworthy; that left to themselves they never would achieve the goals they ought to or that society expects of them. They fear the basic purposes of students and believe that students must be *made* to learn the right things, at the right time in the right ways no matter what. They point to horrible examples of what can happen when teachers let students do as they please. In my experience, helping students fulfill some of their needs in school does not require that teachers abnegate their responsibilities; neither does it require that society's goals for students be rejected or ignored.

I see my role in teaching as a kind of helper-catalyst: aiding students on one hand, to understand the world they live in; and on the other, helping them as best I can to achieve maximum personal growth while they remain in my field of influence. In the interaction of students with society and the world, I try to act both as a friend of students and at the same time as a friendly representative of society. In the remainder of this chapter, I have tried to set down six areas in which my beliefs about educational and societal goals affect my thinking and practice.

Creating Environment

A large part of the academic curriculum is devoted to helping students understand society, directly, in social studies classes or such subjects as sociology, history, civics, anthropology, or political science; and indirectly through subjects like mathematics, reading, writing, composition, and many more tool or skill subjects designed to equip students with techniques for coping with modern life. Formal courses are hardly enough, however. As we have seen in earlier discussions, experiential learning is far more likely to affect behavior than mere exposure to information. Schools represent a significant portion of the student's immediate society. They are also institutions of the larger society and ought to project the very best aspects of that society in action. Teachers, administrators, other students, school organization, curricula, practices, and atmospheres are what students experience in school. They ought, therefore, to represent the best of societal purposes and values in operation. I believe it is the responsibility of *every* teacher, not just social studies faculty, to contribute to that end.

Responsibility is never learned by having it withheld. Responsibility is learned, like math or any other subject, by success experience at simple levels followed by increasingly difficult problems paced to student readiness and capacity. It requires confronting problems, making choices, being involved in decisions, taking the consequences of one's actions, learning from mistakes—not with respect to artificial problems, but real ones, relevant to the world of current experience and one's relationship to it. Responsible citizenship, like any other responsibility, is learned in the same fashion—by having opportunities to practice it.

To provide such opportunities in my classes, I try to convey as early as possible how I see my role as teacher and what I expect of students. After that, each student is left as free as possible to make personal decisions about goal priorities, how to tackle the semester's work, what resources to use in the process, and how to demonstrate progress and achievement. Other opportunities to operate democratically are provided by continuous opportunities for class or group decisions, interaction with the instructor, and cooperation with other students. To do this successfully, I find, it is necessary to clearly define the parameters within which choices and decision can be made, then stick by them faithfully. Nothing so quickly destroys trust, involvement, and acceptance of responsibility as telling students, "You can do this or that," then when the "chips are down" rejecting decisions or standing in the way of their being carried out. This happens all too often with student government. Students are told they can govern themselves, but the limits of decision making are not clearly established. Then, when decisions are made, the faculty or administration finds it necessary to veto student efforts. Result—students get the message, "Our student government is only a game." After that they treat it as a game while the faculty piously wails, "They don't even treat their own student government as though it were serious!" little comprehending that the faculty itself taught students so.[6]

A major roadblock to creating environments for responsibility and democratic action is the pathological fear of making mistakes that seems to characterize the thinking of many teachers and administrators. Students are robbed of valuable learning opportunities by educators preoccupied with "being right." Fearful that students may make mistakes, they do not dare give students freedom to try. Many of our most valuable learnings occur as a consequence of making mistakes, taking the consequences, and searching for new and better solutions. Persons afraid to venture are forever locked in the status quo. The essence of creativity is daring to make mistakes. Teachers, afraid that students may make mistakes, are cutting them off from important sources of growth and achievement. To prepare for a future dependent upon successful human interaction calls for schools that confront students daily with significant human problems, where students and faculty are continuously exploring effective interrelationships, where humanistic and democratic goals have high priority and all school personnel are actively seeking to model good human relationships.

Seeking Involvement

Societal goals for the education of youth are not very likely to be achieved until somehow students get involved in the process. Bringing that about is no easy task. When little children first come to school they are sheltered, cared for, and carefully taught the "right" way to do things. They are organized, taught, tested, rewarded, or punished by people who know how things "ought" to be. The same conceptions are often continued clear through to graduate school. The philosophy that the teacher knows and must therefore control and direct never lets up, though students grow more mature and presumably better able to make their own decisions. It is not surprising then that they leave decisions to the "experts" and involve themselves in the learning process only so much as to keep their teachers off their backs.

Psychologists in recent years have called attention to "learned helplessness," a syndrome in which persons believe that what they do will make no difference in changing the world about them. Such beliefs were characteristic in prison camps when prisoners, convinced they were totally powerless to affect their fate, gave up making the slightest attempts to better their conditions. The syndrome appears in persons given little opportunity to try their wings or who have been repeatedly prevented from taking charge of their own affairs by real or imaginary forces outside their control. Many citizens suffer from this condition, resulting in widespread apathy, failure to vote, and general feelings of "what's the use?" The condition is also characteristic of many students who go through the motions required of them in school with never a thought that they could exert a significant influence upon the events about them.

To learn about society and one's own relationships to it requires personal involvement. Responsible citizenship is learned from personal experience, from opportunities to relate to others in increasingly successful ways. It requires social contact and opportunities to learn social skills, to experiment, to think about, and to explore ideas with others. It is learned from cooperation. To overcome reluctance to involvement, I find it helpful to apply the search for barriers technique mentioned in Chapter 5. Beyond that, I make every effort to convince students that they do matter and what they think and feel is important. I freely express my own feeling that there are few right answers in this world, and students are much more capable of finding effective ones for their own lives than outsiders.

Choice, Decisions, and Consequences

Responsible citizenship requires making choices. It is an interesting observation, however, that schools designed to produce such citizens permit more choices and decision to kindergarten and early grade students than anywhere else in the system. As students progress through school they are permitted to make fewer and fewer choices despite increasing age and presumably greater maturity. In the real world people must make innumerable choices and take the consequences. To prepare youth for such a world, it seems to me, schools and teachers should not only provide opportunities for students to make choices, but students should be *required* to make choices and decisions wherever possible—then suffer or enjoy the results.

There are not many possibilities for choice in a lecture-class, but open, discussion, problem-solving, democratic classes can provide almost limitless opportunities. Students can participate in decisions about what to study, when to study, how to tackle it, what to use for resources, how to evaluate progress, and many, many more. Giving students choices is no great trick. Any teacher can do it who believes it is important. Encouraging choice and decisions sometimes makes classes less orderly and upsets teacher control, but I find that a very small price to pay for contributing more certainly to student growth and making classes more fun at the same time.

Real Problems

People do not learn well from make-believe problems. Real responsibility for real problems is far more likely to result in effective learning. Even pretend problems are better than mere talk; and I find that simulation, role playing, even imagining "what might happen if . . ." can often be highly useful. But nothing can quite take the place of experiencing real problems, making decisions about them, and living with the outcomes. It is true that students will not confront some problems of the adult world for years to come. Students are real, however, and the problems they currently face are genuine for them. If we are trying to teach people how to solve problems, any problem will do. Dynamics, cause and effect, principles, values, philosophy, choices of goals and procedures can all be explored in the real problems of students and the society currently around them. With a little ingenuity I find I can relate a great deal of what I teach to the immediate experience of students.

Some years ago I asked a class of young teachers-in-training, "How come students are so uninvolved?" Here are some of the things they told me:

> Nobody believes what we think is important.
> Nobody trusts us.
> All they want is conformity.
> They feed us a Pablum diet—its all chewed over.
> They are afraid to let us try.
> Nobody cares.
> Teachers and students are enemies—they ought to be
> friends.
> It's details, details, details.
> Everyone worries about grades—as though they
> mattered!
> You can't question anything.
> The only good ideas are the old ones—what's in the
> books.

The clincher was this shocker, which everyone agreed was true: "The things worth getting committed to don't get you ahead in school!" Small wonder that students don't get involved. Seen from their perspective, school is a place that deals with things that don't really matter.

In his book, *Fit For Freedom,* Phil Constans comments, "As we go about developing a school environment that is conducive to responsible citizenship, it will be necessary that we take great care to avoid doing anything that makes a farce out of democracy. Let's make absolutely certain that when we say we are involving students in decision-making that this is what we are actually doing. . . . Under no circumstances should we convey to them that they are being involved in decision-making when in fact they are being manipulated and actually are only being given the opportunity to agree with decisions that have already been made. If we can't really involve them in significant ways, let's don't make any pretense of doing it."[7]

Dignity and Integrity of Others

With every increase in modern technology, society becomes ever more dependent on cooperation and responsible interaction of its citizens. Mutual respect for the dignity and integrity of one's fellows is an absolute essential for the successful maintenance and growth of our kind of social order. I believe, therefore, it is the responsibility of every teacher, no matter what his or her subject matter specialty, to help students comprehend the importance of respect for dignity and integrity of others, to model such respect in the teacher's own behavior, and to help students explore the meaning of such concepts in their interactions with each other.

To this end, I try to provide in my teaching numerous opportunities for students to interact with each other in warm, friendly group settings. As group leader I try to set an example of respect and concern for students, their problems, and their opinions. I try to treat students as persons of worth and value. When necessary, I may also stand between students and attacks from their fellows by quietly shifting the brunt of the attack to myself or coming to the rescue of a threatened or beleaguered student. Wherever I can, I bring democratic techniques for discussion and decision making into play. People discover their own dignity and integrity by being treated so. They contribute to the worth of others by treating them so. With that understanding in mind it is a simple matter to select one's methods and techniques to provide such experiences for students.

Implementing Self-Actualization

Each of the four characteristics of self-actualization suggests immediate and obvious courses of action for implementation in
and out of classrooms. Helping students become informed is what
schools are traditionally all about. Teaching our subjects is what we
teachers have been doing for generations and success experience
with any subject matter can be, in itself, an important growth experience. My students have information needs, however, far beyond the
particular area of my subject matter expertise and I try, as best I can,
to be sensitive to those needs, to provide as much information as I
can, and to put them in touch with appropriate sources of further
help.

The remaining characteristics of self-actualization, a
positive view of self, openness to experience, and feelings of identification or belonging, are also self-suggestive but are much less uni-
versally accepted as proper teacher concerns. For me, they are not
only legitimate objectives for professional practice, their achievement
contributes directly to student success in learning the subjects I am
expected to teach. As we have seen earlier, a positive view of self,
openness to experience, and feelings of belonging are vital factors
affecting learning and cannot be ignored in the teaching of any subject.

To implement the characteristics of self-actualization in
teaching does not require fancy equipment, supplies, organization,
procedures, or even special training.[8] What is needed is awareness
of the characteristics of self-actualization, an appreciation of their
importance, and a desire to contribute to their achievement. Positive
views of self, openness to experience, and feelings of identification
and belonging are learned from experience. Applying that principle
to teaching is fundamentally a matter of asking a series of simple
questions. The questions themselves suggest their own solutions.
Here are some I ask myself:

How can a girl feel able unless somewhere she has
some success?

> How can a boy feel he is a person of dignity and integrity unless someone treats him so?
> How can a woman feel acceptable unless someone accepts her?
> How can a man feel he belongs unless someone treats him so?
> How can people feel worthwhile, liked, wanted, or cared for unless someone treats them so?

In the answers I find to questions like these, I discover the things I need to do to forward self-actualization.

CHAPTER 7

About the Future

A prime purpose of education is to prepare youth for the future.[1] To do that successfully requires some conception of what the future will be like. Knowing that, however, is a much more difficult task than it once was. Until recently, the future was fairly stable and educators could make reliable decisions about what students ought to learn with reasonable chance of being accurate. But no more. We are living in the midst of a profound revolution which most people are not even aware exists. In the last thirty to forty years we have catapulted into a time when the futures we face are changing with bewildering speed and shaking the very foundations of our way of life. These are not wild dreams or science fiction stories. They are hard realities already upon us and require great changes in our accustomed ways of thinking.[2]

Trying to predict a rapidly changing future in specific terms is an impossibility. There are, however, a few generalizations that practically all students of the future agree upon and those have enormous implications for education in general as well as for the personal theories of individual teachers. Here are four of them.

EXPECTATION NUMBER ONE: THE
EXPLOSION OF INFORMATION

Almost everyone is aware of how much more there is to be learned today than just a few years ago. One hears frequent reference to the "information explosion," but few of us really comprehend how great the increase in available information is. Here are a few statistics provided by several futurists. Some 90 percent of all the scientists who have ever lived, they tell us, are alive today. Technical information doubles every ten years. There are 100,000 technical journals available now and the number doubles every fifteen years.[3] In my own field of study, doctoral students in 1940 were expected to stand examination in the entire field of psychology. Today, the idea that any one person could have a comprehensive grasp of the entire field of psychology seems totally absurd. Similar explosions of knowledge have occurred in every other discipline, and futurists tell us this is only the beginning. The explosion will continue at even faster rates in the years to come.

The information explosion has made the concept of the teacher as a fountainhead of knowledge ridiculous. Science has provided us with marvelous techniques for the dissemination of information like radio, television, movies, computers, recordings, and many more. These devices are capable of placing vast amounts of information in the hands of almost anyone quickly and efficiently. They have also made the primary role of teacher as information provider obsolete. Today's teachers will frequently find their students better informed than themselves on many topics. Not long ago a kindergarten teacher told me with a sense of shock about a little boy in her class who corrected her space terminology. "Imagine that," she said, "and besides, he was right!"

EXPECTATION NUMBER TWO: THE
INCREASING RAPIDITY OF CHANGE

Few of us are aware of the full significance of the changes going on about us. Futurists tell us, for example, that the speed of communication, transportation, and computation, and the amount of power available to us just since 1945 has increased by figures of ten to the seventh and eighth power over all the rest of human history since man first appeared on earth. The present is changing fast and the future will continue to change at even more rapid rates.[4] There are something in the neighborhood of 90,000 different occupations in our society, and the number keeps increasing. Students coming out of high school today face the prospect that they may have to change their life work four or five times in their lifetimes. The preparation of youth for a world of such rapid change must surely be quite different from that required for a stable, predictable future.

EXPECTATION NUMBER THREE: THE PRIMARY PROBLEMS OF THE FUTURE WILL BE HUMAN ONES

Since man's first appearance on earth, the primary problem has been how to wrest from the environment the food, clothing, shelter, and power required for personal welfare or that of others. With the developments of science over the past hundred years, industry in the past seventy years, and the discovery of atomic power in the last forty years, all that has changed, producing an enormous revolution in the fundamental nature of the problems faced by humankind. Science has given us the know-how to solve the problems of food, clothing, and shelter. Industry has supplied the technological understanding to produce goods and services in enormous quantities, and the discovery of atomic power promises unlimited power to make it all work (or destroy us all). The crucial problems of the past were problems of things; the problems of today and tomorrow are matters of persons and their interactions with one another. We have left the era of the physical sciences and entered the era of the social sciences.

We live today in the most interdependent, cooperative society the world has ever known since the dawn of history. Few of us could live more than a few hours totally out of touch with other people. The more complex and technological the world becomes, the more each of us is dependent upon thousands of persons whom we do not know and have never even seen. To become aware of how very much we are dependent on our fellows one needs but stand before the gleaming racks in a typical supermarket and imagine the number of persons required to supply those things. We could not even drive if we could not count on other drivers to stay on their side of the road. Imagine having to drive in a truly competitive society!

We now have the knowledge and the technology to feed, clothe, and house the entire world, only to find ourselves faced with a new problem—the human one. The major problems we face today and the primary problems we shall face in the future are human ones, having to do with learning to live effectively with ourselves and others. Problems of poverty, ecology, pollution, overpopulation, food distribution, use of energy, war, and peace, health, aging, crime, violence, terrorism, and human rights are all human ones. Even the atomic bomb is no problem in itself; it is the people who might use it we need to worry about.

EXPECTATION NUMBER FOUR: THE SEARCH FOR PERSONAL FULFILLMENT WILL BECOME INCREASINGLY PARAMOUNT

Not only are we thoroughly dependent on other people, but all our technological advances make the world an even smaller place in which the power of individuals for good or evil is immensely increased. Technological advances make us so interdependent that a single person at the right place and time can throw us all into chaos by assassinating a leader, skyjacking a plane, setting off an atomic bomb, pulling the wrong switch in a nuclear plant, holding people hostage, or going berserk in an automobile. Interdependence makes terrorism simpler and more dangerous for ever larger numbers of people. More than ever, societies of the future will be dependent upon caring, responsible citizens, willing and able to pull their own weight. Persons who feel frustrated and alienated from society are a danger to everyone. After all, if you do not feel you are a member of the club, there is no reason to pay your dues or look out for the other members. The personal fulfillment of citizens in an interdependent society is a necessary ingredient for continuing safety and welfare of its numbers.

Even if personal fulfillment were not so essential for the safety of societies in the future, it is destined to become an increasingly important motive for individual citizens. The more we succeed in providing people with satisfaction of basic needs, the more persons are freed to seek the fulfillment of personal goals and aspirations. As Maslow pointed out in his hierarchy of needs (Chapter 3), people cannot advance to higher levels of motivation until lower ones are satisfied. On the other hand, as people's basic needs are fulfilled, they are set free to explore at higher levels of personal fulfillment. From this it follows that the more a society succeeds in providing human beings with goods and services that fulfill basic needs, the more its citizens will seek fulfillment of higher more personal ones like love, self-esteem, and self-actualization. Such turning of attention to matters of growth and fulfillment is not narcissistic. It is a further expression of the basic human need for health and fulfillment I spoke of in Chapter 2. The future we can see from this vantage point seems likely to be characterized by more and more citizens seeking personal growth and development physically, mentally, emotionally, and spiritually.

SOME IMPLICATIONS FOR EDUCATION AND TEACHING

The four cited beliefs about the future have enormous implications for my professional thinking and action. A few of the things they mean for me are as follows.

Intelligent persons — the goal of education. For many years we have been able to plan curricula with the assurance that "these things are essential," but those days are gone forever. Curricula can generally be defined in terms of content, skills, and processes. With respect to content, the information available in the world is so great, change is so rapid, and the future needs of students are so diverse that it is no longer possible to be certain any item of subject matter will be necessary to cope with life even in the very near future. With respect to skills; reading, writing, and arithmetic, at least to the extent of the very early grades, seem likely to be significant requirements for successful functioning for some time to come. But even these can no longer be regarded as vital for *every* student. Television and radio have made it possible for many citizens to get along quite adequately in modern society with very little reading. The typewriter and telephone have done the same for writing and calculators are increasingly employed by everyone, even for such simple tasks as balancing a checkbook. Only the process aspects of curriculum now meet the criterion "essential" to prepare youth adequately for the world they will inherit.

A common curriculum to be required of everyone is no longer a valid goal for education planners. Instead, we will have to concentrate on producing intelligent persons—citizens able to encounter and solve problems that cannot now be foreseen. Tomorrow's citizens must be effective problem solvers, able to make good choices and create solutions on the spot. Since we are unable to forecast the future in specific terms, schooling must be directed toward the production of intelligent persons. To achieve that end teaching must concentrate prime attention on the growth and development of students rather than content and subject matter. This means for me focusing on processes rather than ends, and persons rather than subject matter.

Effective problem solving is learned by confronting events, defining problems, puzzling with them, experimenting, trying, searching for effective solutions. It is a creative process not tied to any particular subject. It is also best learned from confronting *real* problems, not artificial ones. The most real problems people face are personal ones, but in most schools the problems students are asked to confront are rarely personal, and nearly always artificial.

I find myself less concerned with outcomes and more concerned with processes. I no longer spend much time worrying about whether all my students are learning what others think they should. Nor do I place myself under heavy pressure by establishing rigid timetables for achieving subject matter goals. I spend more time on motivation—how to get students involved in the process of learning, "turned on" to the pursuit of ideas and projects. I concentrate more effort on encouraging, helping, facilitating students to confront problems and think about matters relevant to my curriculum area defined in very broad scope. This often seems to take us far afield from the established syllabus and, when I first started teaching this way often made me uneasy about whether it was time well spent. I am struck, however, by the frequency with which such far-ranging explorations turn out to be highly fruitful, not only for problem solving practice but for grasp of content as well. Concentrating on processes also makes it possible for me to operate in more relaxed fashion and students respond by learning more effectively; so much so that levels of performance that once would have seemed extraordinary now seem only normal.

A future of choices requires an emphasis upon values. The world today's students will be moving into is a future of rapid change requiring many choices. To maintain stability in such a world and to stay on track toward valuable and meaningful goals requires a framework of values as a basis for choices. People do not behave much on the basis of facts. As we have seen, they behave according to feelings, attitudes, beliefs, values, hopes, aspirations, and personal meanings. An effective school system cannot ignore so vital a factor in the preparation of youth.[5] Values exploration must be an important objective in the curriculum. This does not mean schools must "teach" values in the sense of deciding what values students should hold, then indoctrinating them. Values are personal, private, internal beliefs derived from personal experience, exploration, and discovery. What is needed are schools that demonstrate positive values in every aspect of their organization and that encourage and facilitate student exploration of values throughout the system.

Some educators have sought to meet the need for values exploration through "values clarification" games. Such games can sometimes be helpful in starting the processes of exploration by confronting students with problem situations involving questions of values. Too often, they go no further and are frequently used by teachers as time fillers—pleasant ways to escape the boredom of "required" business, to get people talking, or to meet the objectives of "affective education." I have occasionally used such games, but I prefer exploration of values that rise in the course of group discussion, confrontation with problems arising in our own community, school, or classroom interactions.

Students live and work in the midst of value problems and much of their growth is concerned with the search for satisfying, defensible outlooks on life. With very little encouragement, I find, they are eager to explore the implications of subject matter, confront social issues, or share ideas and thinking with others if given the opportunity. One only needs to believe such explorations are important, provide the time and opportunity for their occurrence, and demonstrate a willingness to share one's own self and values. Under such conditions, I find the exploration of values occurs under its own impetus with excitement and profit for everyone, including the instructor.

A future of change demands lifelong education. A rapidly changing world requires that opportunities for learning be available at any time problems arise. The idea of schooling "completed" at any age is obsolete for the world into which we are moving. Education for the future must be life-long. Actually, education has already made great progress toward the achievement of that goal. Such programs as community education, community colleges, adult education programs, and a thousand varieties of programs under public or private auspices bring together people with common needs to solve common problems.

If educational opportunities are going to be continuously available henceforth, then, there is no longer necessity for persons to "complete" their education by any particular time. This means two things for me:

1 We do not have to "force" students to learn particular bits of subject matter in any given time period. If compulsory education for young adults has the effect of turning them off from education forever after, the value of life-long education is destroyed. The success of life-long education requires not only that it be available, but also that citizens appreciate its value and are free to make use of what it has to offer.

2 Life-long education means I, too, am under less pressure as a teacher. I do not have to "make" people learn (even if that were presumably possible). I do not have to feel guilty if my classes stray from prescribed pathways from time to time. I do not have to be all things to all people or feel I have closed doors forever upon them if we do not cover everything the syllabus called for. I can carry my students as far as I can while they are with me, then turn them over to explore what others have to offer. I can do my very best teaching with the feeling that, that is enough.

Concentration upon the Human Condition

If human problems are going to be as crucial as futurists assure us then curricula now must concentrate far more attention on the human condition than is currently the case. The social sciences of psychology, sociology, anthropology, and political science were developed to help us understand the nature of human beings and their interactions with each other. These sciences are now almost a hundred years old, but still do not appear in the curriculum of most school programs, except occasionally as elective courses open to high school seniors—if they have good grades in traditional subject matter courses. The contributions of the social sciences cannot be reserved as proper subjects only for the elite. They must be introduced throughout our schools and at every level.

Introducing "courses" to prepare youth for the human problems they will encounter is not enough. I believe that teachers at every level in every subject must take opportunities and make opportunities to help students explore questions of the human condition wherever possible. Basic principles of psychology, sociology, anthropology, and political science can be observed in connection with any subject. Even the very youngest children can explore the fundamental concept that people behave according to how things seem to them or the dynamics of challenge, threat, conflict, or assimilation. I find this easy to do in my own teaching, but I am also impressed with the ingenious ways in-service teachers find to explore these and many more principles from social science. They discover ways to do this not only in the teaching of social studies but in mathematics, science, art, physical education, mechanical drawing, and shop.

The Importance of Personal Need

Earlier in this book we have several times explored the importance of students' personal needs in learning. Now futurists provide a second reason for concern with student personal needs. The search for personal identity and fulfillment is bound to become an ever more pressing concern in a world where people must live, almost literally "in each others laps," and the major problems people face are people problems. Already this search is characteristic of youth. One can hear it repeatedly in their songs. It can also be observed in the tremendous growth of interest in "consciousness expanding" activities, in "self-awareness" movements, and in a hundred varieties of self-improvement programs. Despite the importance of such student needs, the matter is given little more than lip service in most places and students continue to complain that schooling has little to do with the world in which they live. Far too many complain that their educational experience is largely irrelevant. If schools are truly to educate for the future into which our youth are moving, I see no alternative but to make our schools responsive to student needs for personal fulfillment in the present. This is not mere indulgence of youth. Unfulfilled persons make unhappy, frustrated citizens who can become frustrating and destructive to society. Fulfillment in the present is the best guarantee we have for the successful, responsible citizens we need for the future.

For 150 years we have been trying to teach students as though they were alike. We have grouped them, tracked them, grade leveled them, tried to homogenize and organize them into one kind of group or another for administrative expedience. For at least

50 years since we began doing serious educational research, we have also been unable to demonstrate that any method of organizing or grouping is truly superior to any other method or to no grouping at all. It is time we recognized that human uniqueness is a characteristic of the species and cannot be ignored or set aside. It is a fact of life and must be dealt with. The kind of future for which we must prepare young people underlines once more the necessity for personal, individual learning programs.

Social Interaction and Responsibility

The increasingly interrelated society of the future can only operate effectively if citizens can be counted upon to pull their own weight and look out for their fellows. It follows that schools preparing youth for the future must place heavy emphasis upon responsible citizenship and effective human interrelationships.[6] Such goals must be prime considerations for curriculum planning and teaching. Too much preoccupation with subject matter can defeat those goals. Learning responsibility requires confronting problems, making choices, being involved in decisions, taking the consequences of one's actions, learning from mistakes—not with respect to artificial problems, but real ones, relevant to the world of current experience and one's relationship to it. Similarly, effective social interaction requires personal involvement with others. It is learned from social experience and from opportunities to relate to others in increasingly successful ways. It requires personal contact and opportunities to learn social skills, to experiment, to think about, and to explore ideas with others. All these are only additional reasons why my teaching relies so heavily upon group discussion, joint projects, and techniques that involve my students in personal interactions with fellows.

The need for social interaction, however, goes far beyond the techniques I use in classes. If schools really accept the importance of social interaction as a primary goal, it seems to me they must become far more concerned with the problems of the communities students live in. To do this schools will certainly need to move outside their building walls. Breaking down the barriers between school and community has long been advocated by educational theorists, but most schools have hardly begun to implement such ideas. If we truly accept the importance of problem solving as a primary goal, involvement of students in the larger community seems absolutely essential.

My school and class as microcosm.   In a world where human problems and responsible interactions are essential, schools must, themselves, become microcosms of such experience. People are scripted by personal experience. They learn far more permanently by personal experience than from any amount of subject matter. Schools that hope to prepare youth for an increasingly humane future must therefore operate in ever more humanistic fashion. Concern for individuals, respect for human dignity and integrity, cooperative effort, respect for human rights, and caring for others, it seems to me, must become not only matters for students to learn about, but guidelines for action and criteria for educational assessment in all aspects of schooling.

All school personnel must be keenly aware of the side effects of personal actions, teaching practices, administrative behavior, and even organization of programs. People learn most and best from personal experience. The best guarantee we have that persons will be successful in the future is that they have been so in the past. Student experience today is laying the groundwork for behavior in the years ahead. To prepare for a future dependent upon successful human interaction, therefore, calls for schools that confront students daily with significant human problems, where students and faculty are continuously exploring effective interrelationships, where humanistic goals have high priority, and where all school personnel are actively seeking to model good human relationships.

HUMANISTIC EDUCATION: A RESPONSE TO CURRENT NEEDS

We have seen in the first part of this chapter that the kind of future today's youth will encounter calls for educational programs with high priorities on personal fulfillment and responsible citizenship. The move toward such humanistic concerns is not restricted to education. There are humanist movements in psychology, sociology, anthropology, political science, philosophy, medicine, and theology as well. The need for a humanist movement in education is but another expression of a world-wide trend in human thought brought about by our increasing interdependence in a rapidly shrinking planet. If, now, we add to those social forces our new understandings about behavior and learning, the need for a humanist movement in schools becomes even more certain. In Chapter 3 we observed that the causes of behavior lie in people's belief systems, especially their feelings, attitudes, values, hopes, desires, and beliefs about themselves and the world. If that is true, then teachers who hope to make a difference will need to deal with such human determiners of student growth and development. In Chapter 4 we examined the personal, affective view of learning now held by perceptual-humanistic psychologists, including the importance for learning of such human dynamics as self-concept, personal meaning, feelings of belonging, identification, challenge, and threat. Learning, itself, is a deeply human phenomenon.

For all these reasons, it seems clear that education must seek to make its institutions and practices humanistically oriented. But what is Humanistic Education? An ASCD Working Group on Humanistic Education defined it as follows: "Humanistic education is a committment to educational practice in which all facets of the teaching-learning process give major emphasis to the freedom, value, worth, dignity and integrity of persons. More specifically, it:

1   Accepts the learner's need and purposes and develops experiences and programs around the unique potentials of the learner.

2   Facilitates self actualization and strives to develop in all persons a sense of personal adequacy.

3   Fosters acquisition of basic skills necessary for living in a multi-cultured society, including academic, personal, inter-personal communicative and economic proficiency.

4   Personalizes educational decisions and practices. To this end it includes students in the processes of their

own education via democratic involvement in all levels of implementation.

5   Recognizes the primacy of human feelings and utilizes personal values and perceptions as integral factors in educational processes.

6   Develops a learning climate which nurtures both learning environments perceived by all involved as challenging, understanding, supportive, exciting and free from threat.

7   Develops in learners genuine concerns and respect for the worth of others and skill in conflict resolution."[7]

The published report of this commission also includes a Check List for Humanistic Schools, which many teachers and citizens have found useful for assessing the humanistic tone of their local schools.

When I began teaching in 1935 there were very few humanistic teachers around. Today there are thousands and the number keeps growing. They do not fly banners or advertise their allegiances; they are only beginning to develop professional organizations to communicate with each other and to advance their ideas. Many would be surprised to hear themselves described as humanistic teachers. They understand humanist thinking and apply it to their teaching but have never adopted the humanist label. I have even known humanistic teachers who were operating successfully in schools and systems under the direction of autocratic, dictatorial administrators.

Unfortunately there is a good deal of misunderstanding about humanistic education. Some people have equated the movement with the eighteenth-century philosophy of humanism which held that human beings are totally responsible for themselves and cannot look to Deity for guidance and hope. Such doctrines understandably are shocking to deeply religious persons and they have labeled humanistic education as "secular humanism" and sought its elimination from public education. Some citizens, deeply concerned about the quality of public education, see humanistic education as a departure from age old traditions and a neglect of the basics. Others regard the movement as a kind of fad perpetrated by fuzzy minded, soft headed people out of touch with the *real* goals of education. Still others believe humanism is a nice idea but much too soft a concept to prepare youth for the tough world of reality. None of these fears are justified.

The Humanist Movement in education represents only a recognition of the importance of human problems in the world our students will be confronting and an attempt to apply the best we know about how people behave and learn to the problems of teaching.[8] Humanistic education is not a gadget or a gimmick, not a method or a technique; it's not even a way of organizing. It is a set of ideas; an understanding about the human condition, about what people are like, how they behave and learn, and the nature of the problems they face. It is firmly grounded in new conceptions of the nature of the organism, the causation of behavior, and the processes of learning. These are facts of life. They will not go away and they cannot be ignored because they are inconvenient. To do so is as silly as saying, "I know my car needs a carburetor but I'm going to drive mine without one." Methods, techniques, and ways of organizing or administering come and go. Fundamental ideas about people and learning may last for generations.

Humanistic education does not require the surrender of traditional goals and objectives. Quite the contrary. It is a way of making certain that students achieve them. I am not a humanist because I just want to go about being nice to people. I am a humanist because I *know* that when I apply humanist thinking to my teaching, students will learn *anything* better. They will be better writers, readers, mathematicians, farmers, physicians, truck drivers—whatever. Humanistic education maintains that what students experience about themselves and the world is far too important for education to ignore. Instead, such human considerations must be included in all aspects of educational thinking, planning, and practice. I believe that, too. Consequently, I try to put into practice the principles outlined in the ASCD Working Group's definition of Humanistic Education. It is not always easy and I frequently make mistakes. The rewards, however, are great—not only in greater student achievement but in growth for the teacher as well.

CHAPTER 8

About Methods

Early in this book I pointed out that educators have searched for years for right methods of teaching to no avail. Hundreds of ambiguous research results force us to the conclusion that there is literally no such thing as a good or right method that everyone ought to use. Methods are techniques or behaviors we use to put beliefs into action, and each of us behaves in terms of what seems proper, desirable, or necessary to deal with problems confronted.

METHODS ARE COMPLEX AND PERSONAL

One reason why we cannot find widely applicable good or right methods of teaching is the fact that methods must fit. Even the simplest teacher techniques must fit an enormous number of conditions. Here are just a few: They must fit the conditions: the room, time, equipment, supplies, and temperature. They must fit the subject matter in all its complexity. They must fit the students; especially student needs, differences, readiness, rates of progress, previous experience, interests, and physical conditions. They must also fit the teacher; especially the teacher's personality, belief systems, feelings, attitudes, and characteristic ways of thinking and acting.

137

Finding a particular method always right for such diverse conditions is clearly a hopeless task. Even the best of methods suggested by master teachers, writers, administrators, or supervisors must be tailored to fit a particular teacher and whatever conditions he or she is currently confronting. Effective teaching requires professional, creative persons capable of confronting problems and finding appropriate solutions, not only in daily planning but also from moment to moment in response to changes in conditions or opportunities.

Any method may work for some teacher, some place, some time. The effect of a given method, however, cannot be evaluated simply in terms of observable outcomes. As we have seen earlier, what goes on in a classroom can only be fully understood in terms of what the teacher was trying to do and what the student believed happened. Methods used are only symptoms of the teacher's purpose and perceptions, and the student's real response can only be grasped in terms of what the encounter meant to him or her.

Methods must be judged in terms of the messages they convey. Those messages may be very different from what an outside observer might report or even that the teacher expected. I recall, for example, a high school instructor who picked on me day after day. Even now, as I recall his jibes, some of the pain I experienced back then comes welling up once more. I suffered much at his hands but he knew nothing of the anguish I felt. One day he said to me, "Combs, do you know why I pick on you?" "No, sir," I replied. "Because you can take it!" he said. I still remember my astonishment —he thought his method was paying me a compliment!

While the particular methods each of us use are always personal and specific to the circumstances we confront, there are some general principles about methods with far-reaching effects upon the techniques teachers choose to meet their classroom responsibilities. Some of these have to do with the side effects of methods.

SIDE EFFECTS OF METHODS

Methods teachers employ often produce messages capable of destroying intended outcomes or distorting them so as to produce totally unexpected results. Sometimes these may simply be amusing. They may also subvert entire programs or boomerang to destroy the very goals one seeks. A friend, for example, seeking to help poverty stricken people in the ghetto, developed an "adopt-a-block" program in which the city's service clubs were induced to adopt a particular block in the ghetto and provide financial help for neighborhood improvement. He was totally unprepared to find that while the service clubs were willing to make the required contributions, the people in the neighborhoods he was trying to help regarded his program as an insult and would have nothing to do with it.

The side effects of methods are so important that any time a method, program, or innovation is planned, careful attention needs to be given to four basic questions:

1 Is the goal I am seeking the truly important one? Methods are always set in motion to achieve some goal or purpose. But goals and purposes vary widely in their importance for student growth and learning and it is easy to fall into the trap of employing a method that will help one achieve an insignificant goal instead of a more important one. Sometimes this happens because people become preoccupied with immediate goals and fail to perceive the need for techniques leading to longer range objectives. Insisting that a student complete a routine task right now when he or she is fired with interest in another topic, for instance, may destroy priceless motivation.

Several research studies on effective teaching have demonstrated that good teachers generally seek larger, broader goals while poor ones are intent on smaller, narrower ones. Commitment to one technique can blind a teacher to the necessity for another, better one. It is even possible that a method chosen to achieve a smaller outcome can inhibit the achievement of a larger one. Embarrassing a child in order to stop some obstreperous behavior, for example, may have the effect of teaching the child to avoid further contact with the teacher or building hostility to the subject under consideration. The effects of methods must be read in terms of the meanings they produce in the learner.

2 Is the method chosen truly the most efficient one to achieve the desired goal? Teaching techniques are by no means equally efficient. Whatever the method employed, it should provide results in the most effective and expeditious manner with a minimum amount of disruption to other important goals. While methods need to be simple and easy as possible to administer, efficiency must be judged in holistic terms and there will often be times when speed will need to be sacrificed for some other objective. Much valuable learning is destroyed, for example, because teachers move too fast and accept a student's ability to produce "right answers" as sufficient proof that learning has occurred. Being able to repeat a fact and discovering its personal meaning are by no means the same, and true efficiency may sometimes require sacrificing speed for comprehension and permanence.

    3 What are the effects of the method on the user? Whatever methods teachers employ necessarily modify teacher behavior. Methods used to advance student achievement also have the effect of focusing teacher attention, determining purposes, and influencing directions for action. These effects are inevitable. The methods we choose are commitments, not only to action but to the assumptions from which they are obtained. Techniques of management and control, for example, carry clear messages about teacher purposes and desired relationships with students. They proclaim, "I am the boss, I am choosing the goals, and our relationship is that of superior-inferior."

    Methods chosen may also commit teachers to less important goals. One effect of the press for behavioral objectives in the last decade was to concentrate teacher attention upon specific behaviors that could be quickly achieved and precisely measured. This often focused teacher attention so firmly upon simplistic goals that larger objectives of education were neglected. Sometimes methods of teaching are mandated by well-meaning legislators, school boards, administrators, or supervisors who hope thereby to improve educational practice. Often these do little more than increase the frustrations of what is already a demanding task for conscientious teachers. They may even hinder achievement of the very objectives they were intended to fulfill. Recent national assessments of student achievement in mathematics, for example, suggest that an unexpected outcome of the "back to basics" movement is a decrease in student problem-solving abilities. Methods that fence teachers in, inhibit creativity, or create debilitating anxieties may prove to be too great a price to pay.

4   What is the effect of chosen methods on the student? As we have seen, the effect of methods lies in the messages they convey. How students perceive methods and what they learn from their employment must be matters of vital concern in the selection of teaching techniques. Every teacher can name instances in which students received quite different messages from those intended. One needs but read the responses students make on examination papers to find sad or hilarious examples of student meanings far removed from what the teacher intended. Techniques that threaten, destroy self-esteem, distort perceptions about what is really important, or incur negative, hostile behavior may be no bargain when assessed in terms of their impact. Years ago, my son, home from college, expressed great anger at the college grading system. Inquiring about his frustration, he told me, "Dad, grading students on a curve makes it to my advantage to destroy my friends. That's a hell of a thing to teach young people!" Students learn from all their experiences, including the methods teachers use, and those learnings must be taken into account in determining the usefulness of any method.

OPEN AND CLOSED SYSTEMS OF THINKING

Two general approaches for thinking about methods are characteristic of today's schools: a closed system and an open one. Each of these frames of reference has implications which extend to all aspects of schooling. A commitment to one or the other of these basic systems almost inevitably commits teachers and administrators to a whole series of further consequents about philosophy, curriculum, administration, values, and teacher-pupil relationships. To avoid unintended outcomes and assure effective choices of methods, it seems to me, calls for clear understanding of closed and open systems in one's personal theory of teaching.

Closed system thinking begins with some clearly defined objective, chooses the machinery to reach it, puts the machinery in operation, then assesses the outcomes to determine if, indeed, the objective was achieved. This is the approach one would use in establishing an itinerary, producing a product in industry, or teaching a child an arithmetic function. This way of thinking about problems has been very useful in our highly technological society. Closed system thinking also has tremendous appeal to legislators, business people, school boards, administrators, and parents. It is the way of thinking they are used to and seems so logical, straightforward, and business-like that, surely, applied to education it should solve all our problems.

Open systems, on the other hand, often operate without clear-cut goals or objectives. One confronts a problem then searches for solutions—the nature of which cannot be clearly discerned in the beginning. This is the approach counselors use in assisting a client to explore a problem. It is also the system employed in a legislature debating an issue, in a laboratory seeking a cure for cancer, by an artist producing a painting, or in modern "discovery" approaches to teaching. Unfortunately, in our society, open system thinking is far less understood and less often employed than closed systems. It is extremely important for modern education, however, and teachers need to be acquainted with both systems for whichever of these frames of reference teachers use for selection of methods inevitably commits them to a whole series of additional consequences. Some of these are charted in Figure 8-1, but let us examine them a little more closely in the next few pages.

The Focus

A closed system focuses attention on behavioral outcomes, defined in the clearest possible terms and thereafter sought by the most efficient methods for achieving them. Its psychological base is found in behavioral psychology, concentrating on the management of stimuli or consequents to produce desirable behaviors. Teachers operating in this frame of reference are much con-

Figure 8-1.   Open and Closed Systems in Education

Topic	Closed	Open
The Focus	Behavior management, control, or manipulation Based on Behavioristic Psychology	Process oriented—facilitating conditions Based on Humanistic Psychology
Teacher	Expert diagnostician Total responsibility Precise goals or skills Director, manipulator of forces or outcomes	Guide, helper Shares responsibility Broader goals Consultant, aid, facilitator
Curriculum	Oughts and shoulds Right answers Prepare for world Specific goals, grades, and evaluation	Process goals Creation of conditions Problem centered Fill needs, create new ones
Techniques	Industrial model Competition and evaluation valued Administration dominant Emphasis on goal achievement	Personal growth model Cooperative effort stressed Many group decisions Emphasis on intelligent problem solving
Philosophy	Control and direction Great man concept Doubts about motivation	Growth philosophy Democratic Trust in human organism
Students	Passive Teacher as enemy Dependent Lack commitment Conformity Endurance of stress	Active, responsible Teachers as helpers Participate in decisions Involved Creative Concern for others
Values	Simple skills Ends clearly known Conditions for change in teacher control	Broad goals Ends not precisely predictable Humane values

cerned with management and control of students or the events impinging upon them. Motivation in a closed system is primarily seen as what teachers do to or for students to induce them to move toward clearly defined objectives. Objectives may be defined by the students. More often, they are likely to be established by the curriculum, teachers, or administrators. The "behavioral objectives" movement of the 1970s was a prime example of the application of closed system thinking to educational problems.

Open system thinking is a process-oriented frame of reference. It is especially applicable to situations wherein hoped-for outcomes cannot be neatly and precisely defined in advance. As a consequence, teachers concentrate attention on creating conditions conducive to helping students explore problems and discover meaningful solutions. Open system thinking finds its theoretical base in perceptual-humanistic psychology concerned, not only with behavior, but also with the internal attitudes, beliefs, feelings, values, or perceptions that produce behavior. The processes of learning are advanced by encouraging learners and facilitating optimal conditions for learning to occur. Motivation in an open system is seen as an internal matter having to do with student needs, likes, dislikes, and aspirations.

The Teacher

In a closed system all responsibility is lodged in the teacher for seeing to it that ends are properly achieved. The process is similar to the medical model with which most of us are familiar. One goes to the doctor and states his or her problem. The doctor then diagnoses the situation, determines the goals to be achieved, and writes a prescription for the patient who is expected to carry out the doctor's orders. Responsibility for control and direction is almost exclusively in the hands of the doctor, with the patient in a passive or subservient role. The model is also familiar in the structure of modern industry, the military, and many other institutions. Similarly, in a closed system the task of the teacher is to expedite progress toward preconceived goals. To do this well, teachers must be expert diagnosticians who know at any moment precisely what is going on and where events must be chanelled next. Such a view places almost total responsibility on the teacher for defining goals and for achieving them. The teacher's role is that of director or manager responsible for the manipulation of forces or consequences so that preconceived ends will be achieved.

Open systems have a quite different focus of responsibility and role for the teacher. Since end products are not precisely known in advance, responsibility for outcomes is shared by all who confront the problem. This jointly shared responsibility removes a great burden from teachers. They do not *have* to be right. The emphasis in open systems is on participation with sharing of power and decision making. The role of the leader in such a system is not director, but helper or facilitator whose expertise is expressed in the advancement of processes, in creating conditions conducive to learning. The role of the teacher is not to manage, but to minister, to act as helper, aid, assistant, facilitator, or consultant in an on-going process.

The Curriculum

The curriculum, seen from a closed perspective, consists of a body of knowledge, subject matter, information, or skills to be acquired. These are couched in terms of "oughts" and "shoulds," matters defined by society, legislators, administrators, supervisors, teachers, or parents as important objectives of schooling. Most teaching revolves around these objectives; evaluation, competition, grades and various forms of reward or punishment are instituted to assure maximum achievement on the part of students.

Viewed from an open system, the curriculum is also concerned with helping students acquire knowledge and skills required for effective citizenship. Goals are much less precisely defined, however, with opportunities for much diversity and individual choice. Curricula are also more likely to be defined in process terms—problem solving, creativity, responsibility, learning how to learn, or in broader, less precisely defined subject matter objectives.

Because goals are broader and more personal, cooperation is more likely to be stressed and evaluation and grades are less frequently employed. Greater emphasis is placed upon filling individual needs and creating new ones.

Techniques and Methods

The focus of closed systems is on management and control. Consequently, methods chosen by teachers and administrators are patterned after industrial or medical models with control in the hands of "experts" or bosses intent upon the achievement of manifest objectives. Competition and evaluative techniques are highly valued in such a system, with much stress on goal achievement, standards, and discipline. Administrative hierarchies tend to be sharply drawn with clear distinctions between leaders and followers.

Open system methods illustrate a growth model. Like growing a healthy plant, one places the seed in the best soil to be found and surrounds the growing plant with the best possible conditions for growth. In similar fashion, open system methods concentrate on processes and on facilitating optimum conditions for student development. Cooperation between students and teachers is valued and group decisions are frequently manifest. The emphasis is less on learning "right answers," and more on intelligent problem solving.

Philosophy

Closed system emphases on control, direction, and selection of goals by leaders leads in the extreme to a "great man" concept of action. Such a philosophy seeks a "great man" who knows where the people should go while others insure they get there. The position begins with doubts about human motivation and capacity and calls for "people who know" to lead and instruct those who do not.

Operating from a growth philosophy, open system thinking begins with a basic trust in the human organism to find its own best ways and concentrates on creating conditions to make that possible. Its approaches are essentially democratic, recognizing the fundamental dignity and integrity of the organism and the belief that "when people are free, they can find their own best ways."

Effect on Students

Because most decisions are made by teachers and administrators in a closed system of thinking, students tend to be passive, trying to do what is expected. Often they become dependent on teachers for answers and decisions. Teachers may also be regarded as "the enemy," with teacher leadership overtly or covertly resisted. Stress or anxiety are frequent characteristics of students in closed systems. When people do not share in the decisions that affect their lives they tend to conform to the system, break out in rebellion, or leave the field by copping out or dropping out. Students do too.

In open systems teachers are more likely to be regarded as helpers or friendly representatives of society. As a consequence, students are more active and involved in their own learning process. They participate in decision making and are, hence, more likely to be cooperative and responsible. With emphasis upon problem solving they are more likely to be creative than conforming. Tension levels are also likely to be at lower levels in open systems and characterized by greater concern of students for one another.

Values

In the preceding paragraphs we have delineated very sharply between closed and open systems of thinking and their implications for educational practice. I have made this sharp contrast intentionally for the purpose of outlining the two positions. It should be recognized, of course, that such clear distinctions ordinarily do not appear in daily practice; rather, teachers may be found operating in one or the other frame of reference as occasions demand. This is as it should be. Each of these ways of approaching problems has important values to contribute to one's overall teaching theory. The point is not to adopt one or the other position exclusively, but to utilize each in terms of its unique usefulness.

There is a place for management techniques and closed system thinking provides us with the theoretical framework for using them effectively. Closed system thinking or behavioristic approaches can be highly useful, especially when outcomes can be clearly and simply defined and where teachers are in a position to control the stimuli or consequents of student behavior. These conditions may often be present in classrooms, especially in connection with teaching of specific skills or precisely defined behaviors.

Open system thinking is especially useful for the attainment of broad educational goals or when ultimate goals cannot be spelled out in highly specific terms. It also has special usefulness when we are concerned with producing some change in student inner experience, in feelings, attitudes, beliefs, values, and personal meanings.

SOME METHODS IMPLICATIONS

When I started teaching in 1935 my methods were almost exclusively drawn from closed system thinking. In those days I felt a great responsibility that students learn my subject matter skills. I saw my task as one of instilling ideas and information. I rarely chose my methods from an open system. Students looked upon me as an authority figure and I enjoyed that role. I also suffered a lot because my students frequently did not learn the things I was so anxious to convey to them. I spent a lot of time on the enforcement of rules, requirements, lecturing, testing, and sometimes with discipline problems. I loved my subject and I thoroughly enjoyed teaching it, which probably made up for a good many errors in strategy and tactics. I would not, I could not, however, go back to those ways of teaching today.

Over the years I have moved more and more frequently to open system thinking as the major basis for most of my teaching. I still use closed system techniques and procedures where they are appropriate but find that occurs less and less often. Most of my teaching these days grows out of open system thinking. Partly that is because the subjects I teach and the programs I am responsible for are only partly dependent upon acquisition of specific skills or information. Much more of my teaching calls for helping students discover themselves and effective ways of interacting with their personal and professional worlds. Becoming effective teachers, counselors, psychotherapists, administrators, and good human beings is not so much a question of possessing information or specific skills as a matter of learning to use one's self effectively in whatever helping task one may be engaged in. More often than not, that calls for open system thinking as a basis for the development of professional training programs, for helping students acquire experience or develop appropriate belief systems for the professions they are preparing to enter.

A second reason why my present teaching is largely predicated on open system thinking is that open approaches are more consistent with my personal belief system. A perceptual frame of reference for understanding persons, humanistic approaches to learning, emergent concepts of human need, and the very personal characteristics of human growth and development all seem to me to require open system thinking for appropriate implementation. Such thinking also seems to me more congruent with the demands imposed on education by the nature of the future we human beings are facing.

I find putting open system thinking to work in daily practice pays big dividends in student response and achievement. It also fulfills my own needs both personally and professionally to a far greater extent than my earlier experience with closed system thinking. Operating from open systems I am more relaxed and at the same time more effective, while students are more often "turned on" by my subject matter and respond with enthusiasm to learning tasks. My classes are also more relaxed and informal and the productivity of students frequently amazes me. I enjoy the role of helper, aid, and facilitator much more than the authoritarian managing, directing roles characteristic of my closed system days. My students learn much more and so does the instructor. In my early days of teaching I gave out a great deal of information, so much in fact that there was little time left to take more in. As I work in the more cooperative fashion of open systems, I find my own learning is increased, in part by contributions from students and in part by responding to student needs and questions—a process that keeps my thinking alive and active. Many of my very best ideas have sprung into being as I responded to students' questions or was forced to re-think a position in simpler, more explicit terms.

Open system teaching is not always easy. Education in our country has been couched traditionally in closed system terms and many current attempts to improve education begin from closed system assumptions, for example, behavioral objectives, competency-based instruction, back-to-the-basics. Closed system methods are also so common in our society that they become ingrained in the experience of almost everyone. They are immediately understood and seem so logical, so "right" that they are seldom questioned when applied to educational matters. This raises a problem for teachers using open system thinking. Because such methods are "different," less structured, and especially because students are given much freedom of choice and action, outside observers often become fearful that "things will get out of hand" and students will not really learn under such conditions. Such fears may then be expressed in a wide range of opposition from unspoken disapproval to outright condemnation. Such reactions can be painful experiences for innovators, but the idea that there are no universal good or right methods of teaching—that methods must fit the user—has helped me take such disapproval in stride. It helps me deal with skepticism and a lack of understanding about my methods and what I am trying to do.

It's All Right to Be Me!

The idea that there are no universal good or right methods for teaching—that methods must fit the user—is a very important one for me. I have tried on occasion to be like other teachers without much success. I have also suffered feelings of impotence or guilt because I could not seem to use successfully some "good" method suggested by the experts. Some of my colleagues are possessed of warm, outgoing personalities and characteristically work with students in an atmosphere of effervescent camaraderie. Often, when we are team teaching, I wistfully observe their delightful relationships with students and wish that I could teach in similar fashion. I am basically a shy person, however, and cannot behave exactly like my colleagues. My style is more subdued and intense. This used to worry me. But, if methods are unique, personal attempts to solve problems, then the methods I adopt or invent for myself can be good or right for me no matter what others may do or think. I do not have to be like anyone else to be a good teacher. It is all right to be me! The recognition that my methods ought and should be different from those of my colleagues helps me keep perspective. That is both a relief and a release of energy to experiment and try new things without fear of what other people may think.

Now and then, well-intentioned administrators, legislators, or state departments of education make the mistake of attempting to mandate teaching methods.[1] Since the methods teachers use must be highly personal, such impositions frequently backfire and raise more problems than they solve. When teachers attempt to use methods imposed upon them or methods that do not fit, they do so tentatively, halfheartedly, or contemptuously. Such attitudes are almost certain to result in failure, if not because of the teacher's reluctance, then because the negative messages delivered to students can be counted upon to produce counterproductive student behavior.

To be successful I need to acquire a personal storehouse of methods right for me. I do not have to learn the approved methods of some expert. Instead, I can approach the selection of methods like passing down the cafeteria line in a restaurant, looking at techniques available then picking and choosing what I think might fit my teaching problems and me. Or, I can even decide to leave traditional techniques behind and experiment with brand new ways of working. This is not to say I reject the methods of others out of hand—only that I regard them as suggestions rather than prescriptions and reserve the right to accept them, adapt them to my own needs, or decide not to use them.

For me, the criteria for the appropriateness of any methods must be:

1   Does it fit my personal theory? Is it consistent with my beliefs about human nature, human growth and development, my concepts of learning, the purposes of students, of society, or me?
2   Are the messages conveyed by the methods I use what I intend or can accept? Are the meanings produced in those I interact with in congruence with my fundamental purposes?
3   Does it work? Is it sufficiently successful to be worth continuing?

Keeping Perspective

This concept of methods has made me increasingly leary of "canned" or manufactured materials and techniques for teaching. Industrial organizations have discovered that educational budgets are a promising field for exploitation, and recent years have seen a great burgeoning of methods, techniques, materials, gadgets, and gimmicks marketed as teaching aids. To mass produce methods or materials, almost of necessity, requires standardization, whereas effective teaching seems to me to be a creative problem-solving activity. This is not to suggest that canned materials, gadgets, gimmicks, or programmed techniques cannot be used in creative ways—of course they can be and are so used by creative, problem-solving teachers. Unfortunately, canned materials are also seductive. They are often so neat, available, and simple to use that it is easy for teachers to slip into using them mechanically. For example, vast quantities of mimeographed materials produced to "individualize instruction" often become little more than standardized busy work. Similarly, values clarification games degenerate into convenient time fillers and standardized tests or diagnostic materials fill school files and storage rooms to overflowing without being used.

Educators are great faddists. We keep hoping some method, gadget, technique, way of organizing or administering students or teachers will solve our problems. When I started teaching it was the Palmer method that was going to save us. Since then it has been phonics, languages in the early grades, the new math, the new science, teaching machines, television, audio-visual devices, teacher aides, open schools, open classrooms, and, most recently, behavioral objectives, competencies, computer-based instruction, and back-to-basics. Each of these fads seems to run a course of six or seven years, after which it is replaced by a new one. Meanwhile, nobody notices that the old one died because everyone is off on a new expedition.

Understanding the individual, personal character of methods helps me keep perspective in the midst of the excitement and pressures associated with each new movement. Education is an enormous enterprise encompassing something like 200 million students and 20 million teachers. Nobody is going to change that much by gadgets or standardized methods, not even by legislative fiat or administrative mandates. In the final analysis, education will only be changed as teachers change. That means me and my colleagues in the classrooms, laboratories, and field experiences. It also means I have a professional responsibility to search for new and better ways of operating the schools I am in and the classes I teach.[2]

The Need for Innovation

Even the best of methods in time grow stale for teacher and student. I am convinced that a major cause of teacher burn-out is the failure to innovate and to seek new, more interesting or efficient ways to teach. I need to be continuously engaged in the search for methods more appropriate to my beliefs, my students, my purposes and capacities. To do this successfully, I find it necessary to come to grips with two common fears that get in the way of experimenting with new methods: the fear of making mistakes (mentioned earlier) and the fear that "they" won't let me.

The fear of making mistakes characteristic of our educational system is a tremendous roadblock to innovation and creativity. When people are fearful of making mistakes, creativity stops and innovations do not occur. Exploration and experimentation with new ideas, concepts, and methods requires a willingness to risk, to move into new territory. When teachers and administrators become afraid to make mistakes, education is doomed to endless repetition of the status quo. The growth and development of youth is a change process; so is learning a process of change. But students surrounded by faculties fearful of change are likely to follow suit by finding ingenious ways to "play it safe."

Fear of mistakes not only inhibits innovation; it also undermines the confidence of teachers in themselves. A case in point: For a time, in the 1950s, an exciting movement called "action research" appeared in American education. The idea was that *every* teacher was a researcher and *every* teacher could and should be involved in some sort of experimentation in his or her classroom or school. The movement unhappily died with the arrival on the scene of "research experts" familiar with sophisticated statistics, computers, and esoteric research design. Teachers everywhere were made to feel incompetent to carry out even the simplest kinds of research and before very long action research disappeared like the dodo. To avoid the "fear of making mistakes" trap, I try to adopt an attitude that it is good to look, fun to try, and I *expect* to make mistakes.

They Won't Let Me

A second hazard to innovation is the common complaint that "they won't let me." Often, the "they" referred to is no more than a figment of imagination. As a school consultant, I have often heard teachers complain that administrators, supervisors, or parents would not permit them to try some new thing. Later, when I had an opportunity to speak with these inhibitors, I would find them astonished at the belief they would interfere or reject teacher ideas for improvement. Sometimes the belief that they won't let me may also be a handy rationalization to excuse inaction. After all, who can blame me for maintaining the status quo if "they" won't let me? Using that excuse I can even do nothing and come up "smelling like a rose" as people respond by feeling sorry for me for having to work under such impossible conditions.

Sometimes, of course, the reluctant "they" may be very real. Other people can, indeed, disapprove of the things I would like to try because they are fearful of making mistakes or upsetting the status quo. I have learned, therefore, not to ask permission for the things I would like to try unless it is absolutely necessary. Most people are so caught up in their own problems that they usually do not have time to worry about mine unless I call them to their attention. Within the privacy of my own classroom, I find all kinds of freedom to experiment, change, make mistakes, and try again. People rarely get upset about things I try to do to improve me or my teaching. What upsets them is when I imply that they ought to be or do like me.

A Continuous Search for New Methods

One of the sad things about teaching is that just about the time you get to know a group of students they move on to other things. The fact that semesters, quarters, and terms begin and end is also a great advantage however. One can always start anew. One need not be stuck in the same old rut unless a person likes it that way. To maintain my own mental health and interest in teaching, I find it both necessary and exciting to be continuously involved in some sort of experiment or innovation. I make a practice of periodically discarding old plans, and changing responsibilities, programs, or teaching assignments. This forces me to rethink my techniques or assumptions and in the process I often find new directions to explore while at the same time renewing my enthusiasm for the teaching task.

I believe one reason why many teachers are fearful of experimenting is a consequence of attempting innovations too far removed from current readiness.[3] Elementary teachers are aware of the importance of "pacing" (providing tasks for children at the level of their present competence). The principle holds for adult teachers, too. I avoid innovations too far removed from my present position, which demand too many new skills or call for drastic changes in my personality or way of being. Like everyone else, I work better when I am challenged but not threatened. Accordingly, I choose innovations I am ready for, that I can comfortably handle in steps I can navigate without losing my basic security. Tackling an innovation too demanding or one for which I am not ready is likely only to frustrate me and fail to be of help to my students.

The innovations I choose to try must also be consistent with my personal theory. Sometimes I am intrigued with a procedure demonstrated or described by someone whom I admire or which I have experienced as a participant under someone else's leadership. These I check out against my personal theories of teaching before putting them to the test.

Perhaps the most exciting and growth-producing innovations I have experienced however are those I invent myself in the course of trying to put my theories into practice. This involves beginning with some aspect of personal theory and asking: "If this is so, what then?" Many of the implications of personal theory discussed in this book were determined in just that fashion. Generating innovations this way also has an added value in providing a practical test of the theory from which it arose. If it works, it corroborates the theoretical position; if it does not, it signals the need for possible revision of personal beliefs. One of the most exciting experiences of my professional career came about in just this fashion in a teacher education program at the University of Florida.[4] A group of professors set down a series of basic principles they believed should guide the construction of a teacher education program. After that, we selected ways of working to put our assumptions into practice. Next, we put our ideas into practice by running the program side-by-side with the existing one, accompanied by a research program to determine which was better. Rarely do people approach problems of curriculum change with this kind of orderly, systematic movement from theory to practice. I still regard my participation in that program as one of the most significant contributions of my professional career, and at the same time, one of the most exciting growth experiences in the development of my personal theory of teaching and being.

A great many excellent attempts at innovations in education come to naught because they are not continued long enough. Any sort of change in long-standing expectations is likely to be upsetting to people and cause anxiety. This is especially true when students are confronted with open system techniques. Students have experienced direction, control, guidance, and instruction for most of their lives both in and out of school; so have many teachers. As a consequence, promising innovations are often defeated before they have had sufficient time to prove themselves. The scenario goes something like this: A teacher decides to try something new. Because it is new the teacher feels unsure and so behaves uncertainly and probably makes mistakes. Students in turn sense the teacher's uncertainty and their anxiety is further compounded by the necessity to break old habits and depart from expected patterns. They consequently stumble about and make mistakes, express their frustrations and may even beg to return to "the good old ways." This reaction increases the doubts and anxiety of the teacher to such an extent that he or she decides to go back to what is more comfortable. So, the innovation fails, not because it was a bad idea, but for lack of an adequate chance to be tested and a promising new concept dies aborning. Worse still, it may never be given another chance because the teacher believes the failure was the fault of the methods. In years to come the teacher may still be exclaiming: "No way! I tried that once and it doesn't work!"

CHAPTER 9

About Self

As we have seen, a person's self-concept is probably the most important single factor in determining behavior. This is true for teachers too. What teachers believe about themselves extends into every aspect of their personal and professional lives. For purposes of discussion we can speak of a teacher's personal or professional self. In actuality, these are deeply and inextricably interrelated. Teachers are not always professionals, but they are always persons and their personal self-concepts necessarily affect professional practice, whether teachers are aware of such outcomes or not. Almost any teacher can recall instances when personal problems, involving self, affected classroom behavior as when personal or family matters preoccupy one's attention. Other effects of personal concepts on teaching are less obvious. One's concepts of self as male or female, for instance, have unintended effects on teacher language and behavior as women's lib advocates have helped us understand in recent years.

The reverse is also true. One's experiences as teacher have important effects on broader, more personal concepts of self. One's successes or failures, for example, can cause a person to feel adequate or inadequate. From student reactions one may also acquire definitions of self as personally likeable or attractive. "People

do not live by bread alone" and teachers, too, need evidence of fulfillment. Teachers who do not find their professional lives fulfilling
are not only likely to be unhappy; they are also likely to be ineffective or destructive in their effects upon the students they teach.
Teaching can make important and positive contributions to one's
personal self. Our professional lives make up a substantial part of our
existence. What a waste if it cannot be made to contribute to personal fulfillment.

PERSONAL ASPECTS OF THE
TEACHER'S SELF

Self-fulfillment or self-actualization, as we have suggested earlier, is a consequence of four primary factors: (1) being informed, (2) positive views of self, (3) openness to experience, and
(4) deep feelings of identification with others. These characteristics
also turn out to be important dynamics in the personalities of effective teachers.

Positive Views of Self

Research on teacher effectiveness indicates that good
teachers generally see themselves in essentially positive ways. They
tend to see themselves as liked, wanted, acceptable, able persons of
dignity and integrity. These are not only qualities of good teachers,
they are also qualities of good persons. Positive views of self are
characteristic of healthy personalities and many of the traits of self-
actualizing persons are also characteristics eminently desirable for effective teaching as well. Here are a few such characteristics of self-
actualization mentioned in the literature: more efficient perceptions
of reality and more comfortable relationships with it; acceptance of
self, others, and nature; spontaneity; autonomy; independence of
culture and environment; freshness of appreciation; feelings of oneness with others; democratic character structure; clear discrimination
of means and ends; unhostile sense of humor; creativeness, openness to experience; having trust in themselves; tolerance of ambigu-
ity; thinks well of self and others; sees his or her stake in others; sees

the value of mistakes; develops and holds human values; knows no other way to live except in keeping with his values. One could enjoy and profit from working with teachers having such qualities.

Positive views of self provide teachers with great advantages for dealing with life in or out of classrooms. They provide basic feelings of security leading to behavior likely to be perceived by others as personal strength and assurance.[1] Persons with positive views of self are likely to be less threatened. With greater self-assurance they can also afford to take chances and are therefore more likely to be innovative and creative. Many of the characteristics of self-actualizing persons listed in the preceding paragraph are a consequence of positive feelings about self. In addition, studies on effective and ineffective teachers have provided us with empirical evidence that positive views of self clearly distinguish good teachers from poor ones.[2]

Openness to Experience

The openness to experience characteristic of self-actualizing persons also seems highly desirable for both personal and professional aspects of teacher personality. People who are open to experience are likely to have better relationships with the world around them. They are more receptive, aware, and sensitive to their surroundings. These are important qualities for teachers, whether as persons or acting in their professional roles. Greater openness provides one with more data and decisions made on such bases are likely to be more intelligent and appropriate than those made on the basis of less information. Several researches show openness to experience and authenticity or willingness to reveal self are traits associated with good teachers, while the reverse of these seem characteristic of poor ones.[3]

Identification and Belonging

Likewise, the feeling of identification or belonging characteristic of self-actualization seems equally significant for the personal and professional lives of teachers. In addition to its importance in self-actualization we have seen how identification plays an important part in the processes of learning—for both students and teachers. Teaching is a deeply human, social activity and persons who feel identified with society and with their professions are far more likely to operate smoothly and effectively than persons alienated from society and from their professions. A number of the common traits of self-actualizing persons are direct outcomes of feelings of identification and belonging. They are also likely to be important factors in effective teaching.

Personal Need and Teaching

In Chapter 2 I outlined my beliefs about the need of all human beings for maintenance and enhancement of self. In several later chapters I spoke of the effect of need on student learning. The significance of need cropped up again in connection with Maslow's hierarchy of needs and the effect of need deprivation on human adjustment and maladjustment. So basic a factor in human personality must also play a part in the success or failure of teachers. Teachers who experience personal fulfillment in their private lives are more likely to behave in smooth, well integrated ways with the people around them in their professional roles. With high degrees of need fulfillment, they are even likely to operate in synergic fashion with their surroundings to produce relationships that are stimulating, therapeutic, and constructive. Deprived persons, on the other hand, are likely to be personally unhappy and so deeply involved in seeking personal fulfillment as to have little time or energy to devote to the need satisfaction of others.

Changing Self-Concept

If the self-concepts of persons are so important for human personality and behavior, we need then to ask how self-concept can be changed. Self-concepts are learned beliefs about self. They are acquired like any other learnings and are therefore open to change or modification. That is not to say that self-concept change is either quick or easy. Less important or peripheral aspects of self may be altered fairly easily. Highly important or central beliefs about self, once established, are much more difficult to change. One's conceptions of self as male or female, for example, are such crucial aspects of self and adults have lived with them so long that change is well nigh impossible. Fortunately, most of our self-concepts are not so firmly established and many quite central aspects of self are subject to change in most people.

By all odds, the most important ways in which people learn their self-concepts is through some sort of personal experience. People learn that they are liked, for example, by being liked; that they are acceptable by having been accepted; that they are able from success experiences; or that they are persons of dignity and integrity from having been treated so. The most effective way to produce a change in self-concept is also through some form of personal experience. This is usually much simpler to arrange when one is seeking to help someone else than when the object of change is one's self. Teachers can influence a child's surroundings in such fashion as to assure a child success experience. They can also treat students in ways to help them feel better about themselves. Changing one's personal experience as an adult, however, is another story. Few of us have direct control over the nature of our personal experiences with the world about us. Whether we are liked or disliked, succeed or fail is often dependent upon people or circumstances beyond our personal control. While few of us have complete control over the feedback we get from the outside world, we are by no means helpless. There are things we can do to make our surroundings more positive. Likewise, our experiences with other people are relationships and that means we have something to say about our half of the encounter. By taking full advantage of the available room to maneuver, it will often be possible to exert considerable influence over the kinds of experiences we have with the world about us.

A second but much less potent way of changing self-concept may come about through vicarious experience like drama, reading, or some form of the visual arts. Such experiences may plant a seed, make a suggestion, or possibly start a train of thought. In time, especially if corroborated by personal experience, that may produce significant changes in self-concept.

A third road to change may be found in some form of personal confrontation. Change in a concept of self may be instigated by some event that causes a person to come face to face with the realization that a belief about self is not true. If such a confrontation then stimulates further exploration of perceptions, self-concepts may begin to change in new directions. Encounter groups, counseling, and various forms of psychotherapy are especially designed to produce such confrontations. They may and do occur in the course of ordinary life experience as well. Such personal explorations can be extremely helpful in starting the process of change in self-concept. In the final analysis change is not likely to be very permanent unless it is also buttressed by real personal experience.

Because self-concept is so important an aspect of human personality, many people have assumed that the way to change it is to concentrate attention on it directly. Accordingly, one can find all manner òf tests, games, and questionnaires designed to aid in "self-analysis." Intensive self-analysis is also advocated by supervisors, institutions, and efficiency experts as the path to improved performance in many lines of work. Some schools of counseling and psychotherapy are also deeply influenced by such thinking. Self-concept, however, is not something one "thinks up" or invents. It is learned.[4]

Even when confronted intellectually, self-concept must still be corroborated in real experience if it is to have any degree of permanence. My clients in psychotherapy, for example, do not get well by examining their self-concepts directly. They get better as they explore their personal feelings about the "out there." If I wish to make myself a more lovable person, the thing for me *not* to do is sit around and think about my loveableness! Rather, I need to explore how I feel about the people around me, my friends, husband, wife, lover, people I work with, associate with, care about. As I learn to feel better about these people, I behave better toward them. They, in turn, discover I am a nicer person and treat me as though I were. From this feedback I discover one day that I am a more lovable person. I did not get there however by analyzing myself. What is needed for change in self-concept is change in self-experience brought about by feedback from the "out there."

THE PROFESSIONAL SELF

A profession is a vocation requiring special knowledge or skill. The thing distinguishing it from more mechanical occupations is its dependence upon the professional worker as a thinking, problem-solving human being. The effective professional worker is one who has learned how to use his or her self, knowledge, and skills effectively and efficiently to carry out his or her own purposes and those of society.[5] Professional responsibility does not demand a prescribed way of behaving. It demands responsible approach to professional problems. Emphasis is not on guaranteed outcomes but on the defensible character of what is done. Doctors, for example, are not held responsible for the death of a patient. What they are held responsible for is being able to defend in the eyes of their peers that whatever they did had the presumption of being helpful when it was employed.

Whatever professional workers do must be for some good and sufficient reason, defensible in terms of established theory, rational thought, informal or empirical research, relevant experience, expert opinion, or some other reasonable and substantial basis. Teachers, too, must be prepared to stand this kind of professional scrutiny. To meet such criteria teachers need the strongest possible personal systems of beliefs. Accurate, comprehensive, congruent personal theories will not only provide effective guidelines for daily action, they also provide a rational basis for justifying action or supporting one's professional stance. As a consequence, teachers are more likely to be regarded as accountable, confident persons who "know what they're talking about."

Accountability

For what can teachers be held accountable?[6] Surely not for the behavior of students five years from now; too many others have had their fingers in that pie. Teacher influence on all but the simplest, most primitive forms of student behavior, even in a given classroom, cannot be clearly established. As children get older, less of even those few items can be laid at the teacher's door. The attempt to hold teachers responsible for what students do is, for all practical purposes, well nigh impossible.

Even if this were not so, modern conceptions of the teacher's role would make such an attempt undesirable. Increasingly, teaching is understood, not as a matter of control and direction, but of help and facilitation. Teachers are asked to be facilitators rather than controllers, helpers rather than directors. They are asked to be assisters, encouragers, enrichers, inspirers. The concept of teachers as makers, forcers, molders, or coercers is no longer regarded as the ideal role for teachers and the position is firmly buttressed by evidence from research. Modern thinking about teaching regards it as a process of ministering to student growth rather than a process of control and management of behavior.

While teachers cannot be held accountable for the specific behaviors of students, it seems to me they can reasonably be required to meet five basic criteria:

1 Command of their subject matter
2 Concern for the welfare of students
3 Understanding the nature of human behavior and the processes of learning
4 Possession of clear and defensible purposes
5 Use of methods clearly consistent with the educational purposes they seek to achieve.

To be accountable in such terms requires professional workers with clear conceptions of what is truly important. Without such guidelines people become the victims of circumstance and find themselves riding a merry-go-round like this: Because I don't know what's important, everything is important. Because everything is important, I have to do everything. Other people see me do everything, and then they expect me to do everything. This keeps me so busy I do not have time to think about what is important! Such vicious circles have been the downfall of many a well-meaning teacher or administrator, and the trap is an easy one to fall into. One safeguard is the kind of personal theory we have been advocating.

Personal theories that provide trustworthy guidelines for making adequate choices about what is truly important are: (1) comprehensive, (2) accurate, (3) internally congruent, (4) personally relevant, (5) appropriate to the tasks confronted, and (6) continuously open to change and improvement. They also provide the "reasonable bases" for action required for professional responsibility.

Teachers Are Important

An important aspect of my professional self is a belief that teachers are important. Many teachers do not believe that. There are powerful forces both in and out of the profession that contribute to teacher "put downs" and undermine teacher confidence in their professional significance.

One frequently hears teachers discount their contributions to student growth with comments like: "It's hopeless." "The odds are too great." "What can you do with a child from a home like that?" "How can I compete with television?" "I have my students for such a short time." "Parents (or the community, government, society, or even other teachers) tear down everything I try to accomplish." I believe such comments are based on too gloomy a picture of teacher influence and worth.

Psychologically, we know that every human being is the product of all his or her experiences—from conception to the present moment. This means that any good experience one person provides for another is for all time. Students cannot *unexperience* what they have experienced, so any good thing a teacher does with a student is forever. I find it helpful to think of students like a bank account to which some people make deposits and others withdrawals. My task is to make certain my own activities are deposits. In addition, I can use whatever influence I have to encourage others to make contributions and to avoid withdrawals. It is true that a single experience I provide may not be enough to completely reverse many bad ones, but neither is it ever in vain. Even a holding operation in the life of a child, when everything else is pushing him or her downhill, may be an extremely important contribution. Helping a child to stay as bad as he or she is when everything else about the child is conspiring to make him or her much worse is a contribution many good teachers make without ever knowing it. Time spent in school is a sizeable chunk of a student's life and teachers determine the nature of its impact. What teachers do is not unimportant. Good experiences are forever.

SOME IMPLICATIONS FOR PERSONAL GROWTH

Applying what we have observed about self-concept to personal fulfillment results in five objectives for my personal life.

1   Maintenance and improvement of health.   My physical body provides the house I travel around in and its condition vitally affects the freedom I have to seek for self-fulfillment. I have learned, therefore, to value it and keep it in the very best shape I can. I have not always done that. In years past I have often taken my physical body for granted and have been insensitive to its needs. As a consequence, I have been surprised or hurt when now and then it "let me down." One of the significant social phenomena of our times is the surge of public interest in personal health. All sorts of information and opportunities are now available to guide and help people grow toward high-level wellness. Like millions of fellow Americans, I have discovered it pays big dividends to keep my body in the best possible condition. To that end, I am learning to listen to my body, to respond to its needs, and to spend the time and effort required to keep it in the best shape possible.

2   Positive experience of self.   While one cannot directly think the self into positive views, it is often possible to put one's self in the way of positive experience. Positive selves are acquired from success experience. By entering encounters likely to be challenging rather than threatening, I enhance my chances of success and so of improving my self-concept. By the same token, I avoid encounters likely to be traumatic. When I cannot, I try to find support in congenial company. I find no virtue in the old adage that "failure is good for the soul." I find it better to deal with hard things when I am ready and so have better chance of success. The more success I experience, the more positively I feel about myself. This raises my thresholds for action so that I am more frequently challenged and less often threatened.

3 Identification and belonging. The feeling of oneness is an important characteristic of self-actualizing persons. It is also a feeling I can actively cultivate by cherishing friendships, by getting involved with persons or groups with goals and interests similar to my own, and by valuing opportunities for intimate relationships and communication with others in nonthreatening, warm human encounters. Love is essential for promoting the growth of human beings. Unhappily, it cannot be demanded or achieved by "hard work." One can, however, increase one's chances of being loved by developing sensitivity, demonstrating compassion, and caring for one's fellow human beings. I find a feeling of oneness with others is a source of personal strength and I value and seek it in whatever ways I can.

4 Openness to experience. There are many things I can do to make myself more open to experience. In part, it has to do with good health, positive views of self, and feelings of security and identification we have already mentioned. Such feelings immensely increase my internal strength. They also permit me to confront the world with spirit, anticipation, and a minimum of defensiveness and self-protection. It is also encouraged by the attitude that "it is good to look and fun to try." With such an attitude I can welcome dialogue with people and interaction with events. This helps me be more open to experience and clarifies my perceptions so that I am less likely to be reacting to my own illusions but to events as they are.

5 Getting away. One of the things I have observed as a psychotherapist is that the best counselors I know do not counsel full time. Intense personal involvement, no matter how fulfilling, is also exhausting. Helping professions, done well, require intense concentration. Concentration is a two-edged sword; it focuses attention on the task at hand, but it can also narrow one's vision and so blind us to broader frames of reference. I find it necessary for my own growth and development to get away from my teaching-counseling duties on frequent occasions. I do this not only for rest and relaxation, but also because it provides opportunity for new perspectives and exposure to new experience. The values of getting away are not restricted to yearly vacations. There are equally important dividends in getting away for shorter periods—going to a movie, having lunch at a different place, going to see an intriguing event, spending an hour with a child feeding ducks at the park. Whatever the break, getting away can provide important release and enable return to one's tasks with new viewpoints and challenge.

SOME IMPLICATIONS FOR PROFESSIONAL GROWTH

Applying the above beliefs about the teacher's self to my professional practice, I begin by trying to live up to the five requirements stated for accountability:

1 To be in command of my subject
2 To be honestly concerned for the welfare of students
3 To keep up to date on understanding persons, their behaviors, and the nature of learning processes
4 To be clear about my purposes
5 To select methods of teaching consistent with my best beliefs about teaching.

That is quite an order in itself. Beyond that I would list six other goals.

1 *Acceptance of myself and my students.* I try to accept who I am as I am. I expect me to do the best I can whatever the professional task I am engaged in. I believe that when I

have done the best I can with what I have where I am, nobody can ask any more of me. I also try to extend that principle to my expectations of students. I do not feel I have to love all my students; nobody can *make* himself or herself love someone. I do not feel I "owe" students love. What I owe them is my very best professional effort. That is my prime professional responsibility. If I love them in addition, and I often do, that facilitates teaching and adds enormously to its satisfactions.

When I feel released from the responsibility for *making* students learn or the necessity for delivering students neatly molded in some preconceived model, I can work in more relaxed fashion and accept my students more completely. This frees both of us to determine what is truly important, to set our goals accordingly and to get about the business of making as much progress as we can in the time we are together. Operating in this frame of reference, I am continually surprised by the commitment students make to the task, the hard work they expend in the process, the progress they make, and the creativity they display.

2 Deciding what's important.   A major source of frustration and wasted energy in our profession is brought about by failure to determine what is truly important. I have suffered the exhaustion of its wasted effort too many times in years past. I have also sat through innumerable meetings devoted to trivial questions and listened with patient boredom to "learned discourse" about things that don't really matter. I have even been an active participant in such fruitless endeavors for lack of having decided what was truly worth exploring.

I try not to fall into such traps any more. I cannot be all things to all people. Life is too short and the important problems of education and teaching are too pressing to spend much time on matters of doubtful significance. I try to allot my time and energies to matters of high priority. I avoid discussions of trivia when I can and exercise my rights as a democratic member of the profession to influence agendas and the discussion of professional concerns. Most important, I try to apply the yardstick question, "Is it really important?" to my own planning and teaching. For such decisions my personal theory of teaching stands in good stead. It provides the guidelines I need for making fruitful choices. By relating questions to it, I am better able to concentrate attention on matters of genuine significance. This spares me much frustration and focuses energies on events I can truly influence. It has also made me a better teacher and contributor to the profession.

3 Authenticity.   Research seems to show that good teachers are self-revealing rather than self-concealing. This is consistent with what I have come to value most highly among my personal goals. Above all else, I want to be authentic. That is to say, I want to be real and genuine—who I truly am in my professional life as in my personal life. Psychologists sometimes call that "making one's self visible." Counseling research has demonstrated that when counselors are genuine and openly share themselves with clients, psychotherapy moves more successfully and with greater speed. In my experience authenticity is just as important for the professional relationships of teachers.

Students cannot establish effective relationships with a nonentity. I have to be somebody. My teaching goes best when I am open and willing to share who I am and what I believe with those I live and work with. This does not mean a maudlin dumping of personal problems on students. Neither does it require imposing my values or philosophy. I can and do share my beliefs when they are appropriate. They are also obvious in my behavior to any observer who cares to look. I am neither an indecisive pushover nor a dictatorial tyrant. I respect my personness and integrity and share it openly with students whose personness and integrity also demands my respect.

4 Continuing growth.   In the previous chapter I mentioned the importance of continuous experimentation. I have been an innovator all my professional life. I get bored doing the same things in the same old ways. On the occasion of Carl Rogers' seventy-fifth birthday, the American Psychological Association sponsored a series of sessions at its annual convention extolling Rogers' contributions to counseling, education, and half a dozen other areas. I met the honoree coming from one of these sessions and rushing off to one on new approaches to group experience in which he was participating. "I've never been one to look back," he said. "I find it more fun to explore what I *haven't* done!" I feel much in tune with those sentiments. I need to break out of the status quo on frequent occasions to find new and better ways of thinking and working. I find this necessary, not only to fulfill my professional responsibilities but to replenish my personal needs as well. Some people find innovations upsetting and unpleasant. I enjoy getting into predicaments for the sheer joy of getting out again. I feel very sorry for burned-out teachers listlessly going about their tasks in the same tired fashion year after year. I also feel sorry for their students. A very large portion of my total life span is spent in professional work. What a drag if I cannot enjoy it—or if I cease to grow with it.

In addition to innovations, there are other ways of continuing professional growth. Some of those are reading, attending classes, demonstrations and workshops, travel and observation, but especially through dialogue and discussion with students and other professional workers. I owe a great deal to my students. They have contributed enormously to my personal and professional growth. Nothing is quite so stimulating as the problems I confront in dialogue with bright, inquiring, enthusiastic young people. They pose hard questions and want to explore avenues I never gave thought to before. In our mutual response to each other we each grow. Indeed, I sometimes have a guilty feeling that I've grown more than they and besides I get paid for it!

Dialogue with colleagues may often have similar import but with far less frequency, I find. In a profession dependent upon communication, meaningful dialogue with students is far more frequent than interaction with colleagues. I find it rare in institutional settings for professional workers to get together to talk about things that matter. We get bogged down in politics, institutional affairs, or "housekeeping" matters of organization and administration. Sometimes, too, people "who have arrived" seem to see no need to travel further but spend much time polishing and repolishing the "gems" they already have. The growth producing potential of real dialogue with kindred spirits on a faculty is tremendous, however, and I have learned to value them whenever and wherever they occur.

5   Identification and support.   As we have seen, feelings of identification and belonging are important characteristics of healthy personalities and effective learning situations. They are also important for the growth of teachers. It is hard to maintain high levels of professional practice for very long in isolation. "Everybody needs somebody" the song title goes, and I find I need the feeling of belonging and the support of fellow professionals. I have known schools in which teachers have achieved such extended feelings of belonging that one gets the impression the entire faculty is like one big family. I envy such conditions, but I have never had the pleasure of working in that kind of atmosphere. Wherever I work, however, I seek formal or informal interaction with persons of like persuasion because I need the support and strength such feelings of identification provide. I owe a great deal to colleagues I have encountered in such groups. They have helped me greatly in times of doubt and confusion. They have also provided stimulation for my own ideas and personal growth as well as sheer enjoyment provided by mutual participation in exciting projects and the fulfillment that comes of interacting with warm, caring human beings.

On a broader scale I believe it important for teachers to join appropriate professional organizations. Two kinds of organizations are available in education. One variety is the "housekeeping" group concerned with rules, regulations, standards, ethics, salaries, fringe benefits, and the wielding of muscle to forward professional prestige and status. There is a place for such groups and they need the support of professional workers in order to carry out their functions. They do very little, however, for my personal and professional growth. For that, I need the support and stimulation of "professional" groups like the Association for Supervision and Curriculum Development, Phi Delta Kappa, the Association for Humanistic Education, or other specialized groups devoted to professional dialogue, innovation, and the exploration

of ideas. I believe that teachers who limit their professional affilia-
tions to housekeeping organizations are missing out on the important stimulation to be obtained from interacting with people and
ideas more directly related to professional growth.

6 Keeping perspective. Teachers only occasionally
are able to observe dramatic evidence of their success. Most of us
are full of our subjects and want so much for students to grasp
and appreciate them. But the contributions we make to the
growth of students often do not show until long after students
have left us. Without immediate feedback it is easy to become discouraged. I therefore find the idea mentioned earlier in this chapter that "any good thing a teacher does for a student is forever"
supportive and helpful. It assures me that I am a significant
human being and can make a difference, and that I do not labor
in vain. I am a long way from being perfect, but it is good to
know I have probably been more positive than negative and there
is still a great deal more I can do.

Not only are teachers important; the whole of education is. I believe that much of the greatness of our country is a
consequence of our system of public education. It has been under
heavy attack in recent years. There is also reason to believe it has
not kept pace with the times as we might wish. Nevertheless, it
was a giant step forward when our forefathers brought it into
being. It served us well for generations and still has potential for
important contributions to our American way of life. It is a noble
institution and I am proud to be a part of it.

Another reason for appreciating the importance of
our educational system is the fact that it represents the most significant agency through which we can hope to influence the next
generation.[7] Parents are not organized for the task and the influence of the church continues to decline in our times. Education
is the only organization through which we can hope to reach on-
coming generations in any organized fashion. For many years I
have been a psychotherapist and engaged one way or another in
the training of counselors. Such work is important but essentially
rehabilitative. Satisfying as such work is, it is helping people *after*

they get sick. A much more important task is helping people to grow into healthy, responsible citizens and that is a primary task of education. I am glad I am an educator. I feel I am part of one of humanity's greatest inventions.

Today's problems in education are very great and most teachers want so very much more than we seem to achieve. But change in education is difficult and often maddeningly slow. It is an easy thing for teachers to become hurt, disillusioned, and discouraged. We need to remind ourselves that human resistance to change, distressing as it is, is also the best guarantee we have in a democracy against being taken over by a demagogue. It is easy to lose perspective. Immediate problems seem so urgent. They stand out like sore thumbs and it is easy to get the impression that we hurt all over. As a matter of fact, American education has come a very long way in the hundred or so years since the establishment of public education. Now and then we need to review that progress, lest we get so bogged down in our current problems as to discourage and defeat ourselves. I am keenly aware of the shortcomings in the profession. I know that education can and has made a difference. It also has the potential to make even more.

Endnotes and References

ENDNOTES FOR PREFACE

1. J. S. Bruner, *Toward a Theory of Instruction* (New York: W. W. Norton & Co., 1966).
2. A. W. Combs, D. L. Avila, and W. W. Purkey, *Helping Relationships: Basic Concepts for the Helping Professions* (Boston: Allyn and Bacon, 1978). A. W. Combs, F. Richards, and A. C. Richards, *Perceptual Psychology: A Humanistic Approach to the Study of Persons* (New York: Harper and Row, 1976).

ENDNOTES FOR CHAPTER 1

1. W. J. Ellena, M. Stevenson, and H. V. Webb, *Who's a Good Teacher?* American Association of School Administrators, N.E.A., 1961.
2. A. W. Combs, R. A. Blume, A. J. Newman, and H. L. Wass, *The Professional Education of Teachers: A Humanistic Approach to Teacher Preparation* (Boston: Allyn and Bacon, 1974).
3. Perceptually Oriented Studies on the Helping Professions.

Monographs
Combs, A. W. *Florida Studies in the Helping Professions,* Social Science Monograph No. 37. University of Florida

Press, Gainesville, Florida, 1969. Includes studies by Benton, Dickman, Gooding, Usher, Combs, and Soper.

Dissertations

Brown, Robert G. "A Study of the Perceptual Organization of Elementary and Secondary Outstanding Young Educators." University of Florida, 1970.

Choy, Chunghoon. "The Relationship of College Teachers Effectiveness to Conceptual Systems Orientation and Perceptual Orientation." University of Northern Colorado, 1969.

Dedrick, Charles Van Loan. "The Relationship between Perceptual Characteristics and Effective Teaching at the Junior College Level." University of Florida, 1972.

Dellow, Donald A. "A Study of the Perceptual Organization of Teachers and Conditions of Empathy, Congruence, and Positive Regard." University of Florida, March 1971.

Doyle, Eunice J. "The Relationship between College Teacher Effectiveness and Inferred Characteristics of the Adequate Personality." University of Northern Colorado, 1969.

Jennings, Gerald Douglas. "The Relationship between Perceptual Characteristics and Effective Advising of University Housing Para-Professional Residence Assistants." University of Florida, 1973.

Koffman, R. G. "A Comparison of the Perceptual Organizations of Outstanding and Randomly Selected Teachers in Open and Traditional Classrooms." University of Massachusetts, 1975.

O'Roark, Anne, "A Comparison of Perceptual Characteristics of Elected Legislators and Public School Counselors Identified as Most and Least Effective." University of Florida, 1974.

Swanson, John LeRoy. "The Relationship between Perceptual Characteristics and Counselor Effectiveness Ratings of Counselor Trainees." University of Florida, 1975.

Usher, R. H., and Hanke, J. "The 'Third Force' in Psychology and College Teacher Effectiveness Research of the University of Northern Colorado." *Colorado Journal of Educational Research* 10 (1971): 2-10.

Vonk, Herman G. "The Relationship of Teacher Effectiveness to Perception of Self and Teaching Purposes." University of Florida, June 1970.

Wasicsko, M. W. "The Effect of Training and Perceptual
Orientation on the Reliability of Perceptual Inferences for
Selecting Effective Teachers." University of Florida, 1977.

4. R. L. Curwin, and B. Fuhiman, *Discovering Your Teaching Self*
(Englewood Cliffs, N.J.: Prentice-Hall, 1975).
5. See endnote 3 of this chapter.

ENDNOTES FOR CHAPTER 2

1. A. H. Maslow, *Motivation and Personality* (New York: Harper &
Row, 1970).
2. H. L. Dunn, *Your World and Mine* (New York: Exposition Press,
1956).
3. J. McV Hunt, *Intelligence and Experience* (New York: Donald Press,
1961). A. W. Combs, "Intelligence from a Perceptual Point of View."
Journal of Abnormal and Social Psychology 47 (1952): 662-673.
4. E. C. Kelley, *Another Look at Individualism* (Detroit: Wayne State
University, 1962).
5. Ibid.
6. I. D. Welch, and R. H. Usher, "Humanistic Education: The Discovery
of Personal Meaning." *Colorado Journal of Educational Research* 17
(1978): 17-23.
7. See endnote 3 of Chapter 1.
8. H. P. Constans, *Fit for Freedom* (Washington, D.C.: University Press
of America, 1980).
9. E. C. Kelley, *In Defense of Youth* (Englewood Cliffs, N.J.: Prentice-
Hall, 1962).

GENERAL REFERENCES FOR CHAPTER 2

Rogers, C. R. *Carl Rogers On Personal Power: Inner Strength and Its
Revolutionary Impact.* New York: Dell Publishing Co.,
1977.

Combs, A. W.; Richards, F.; and Richards, A. C. *Perceptual Psychology:
A Humanistic Approach to the Study of Persons.* New
York: Harper & Row, 1976.

Combs, A. W.; Avila, D. L.; and Purkey, W. W. *Helping Relationships: Basic Concepts for the Helping Professions.* Boston: Allyn and Bacon, 1978.
Maslow, A. H. *The Farther Reaches of Human Nature.* New York: Viking, 1971.

ENDNOTES FOR CHAPTER 3

1. D. L. Macmillan, *Behavior Modification in Education* (New York: Macmillan, 1973). C. E. Pitts, ed. *Operant Conditioning in the Classroom* (New York: Thomas Y. Crowell, 1971). B. Sulzer, and G. R. Mayer, *Behavior Modification Procedures for School Personnel* (Hinsdale, Ill.: Dryden Press, 1972).
2. F. C. Goble, *The Third Force: The Psychology of Abraham Maslow* (New York: Grossman Publishers, 1970).
3. D. Snygg, and A. W. Combs, *Individual Behavior: A New Frame of Reference for Psychology.* (New York: Harper and Row, 1949).
4. A. W. Combs, F. Richards, and A. C. Richards, *Perceptual Psychology: A Humanistic Approach to the Study of Persons* (New York: Harper & Row, 1976).
5. See endnote 3 of Chapter 1.
6. See endnote 1 of Chapter 2.
7. V. Raimy, *Misunderstandings of the Self* (San Francisco: Jossey-Bass, 1975).
8. M. W. Lamy, "Relationship of Self Perceptions of Early Primary Children to Achievement in Reading," in *Human Development: Readings in Research,* ed. I. J. Gordon (Glenview, Ill.: Scott, Foresman, 1965).
9. D. E. Hamachek, *The Self in Growth, Teaching and Learning* (Englewood Cliffs, N.J.: Prentice-Hall, 1976). W. W. Purkey, *Self Concept and School Achievement* (Englewood Cliffs, N.J.: Prentice-Hall, 1970).
10. See endnote 3 of Chapter 1.
11. Ibid.
12. E. Kelley, *Education for What is Real* (New York: Harper & Row, 1947).
13. F. C. Luna, and F. D. Cordell, "Humanism: The Vital Ingredient in the Ethnically Aware Classroom." *Colorado Journal of Educational Research* 17 (1978): 15-17.

GENERAL REFERENCES FOR CHAPTER 3

Buhler, C. B., and Allen, M. *Introduction to Humanistic Psychology.* Belmont, Calif.: Wadsworth, 1972.

Combs, A. W.; Avila, D. L.; and Purkey, W. W. *Helping Relationships: Basic Concepts for the Helping Professions.* Boston: Allyn and Bacon, 1978.

Skinner, B. F. *Beyond Freedom and Dignity.* New York: Alfred A. Knopf, 1971.

Walker, J. E., and Shea, T. M. *Behavior Modification: A Practical Approach for Educators.* St. Louis: C. V. Mosby Co., 1976.

ENDNOTES FOR CHAPTER 4

1. See endnote 1 of Chapter 3.
2. B. F. Skinner, *Beyond Freedom and Dignity* (New York: Alfred A. Knopf, 1971).
3. See endnote 6 of Chapter 2.
4. D. N. Aspy, and F. Roebuck, *A Lever Long Enough* (Washington, D.C.: Consortium for Humanizing Education, 1976). D. N. Aspy, and F. N. Roebuck, *Kids Don't Learn from Teachers They Don't Like* (Amherst, Mass.: Human Resource Development Press, 1977).
5. Applying their criteria for effective feedback to grades and grading, it becomes clear that traditional marking systems fail on every count. I have not discussed this question in this volume, but interested readers can pursue the matter in: S. B. Simon, and J. A. Ballance, eds. *Degrading the Grading Myth: A Primer of Alternatives to Grades and Marks* (Alexandria, Va.: Association for Supervision and Curriculum Development, 1976). H. Kirschenbaum, S. B. Simon, and R. W. Napier, *Wad-Ja-Get? The Grading Game in American Education* (New York: Hart Publishing, 1971).
6. M. L. Goldberg, A. H. Passoev, and J. Justman, *The Effects of Ability Grouping.* (New York: Teachers' College Press, 1966).
7. D. Manning, *Toward a Humanistic Curriculum* (New York: Harper & Row, 1971).
8. C. R. Rogers, "The Interpersonal Relationship in the Facilitation of Learning," in *Humanizing Education: The Person in the Process* (Alexandria, Va.: Association for Supervision and Curriculum Development, 1967).

GENERAL REFERENCES FOR CHAPTER 4

Combs, A. W.; Avila, D. L.; and Purkey, W. W. *Helping Relationships: Basic Concepts for the Helping Professions.* Boston: Allyn and Bacon, 1978.
Combs, A. W.; Richards, F.; and Richards, A. C. *Perceptual Psychology: A Humanistic Approach to the Study of Persons.* New York: Harper & Row, 1976.
Cross, P. *Accent on Learning.* San Francisco: Jossey-Bass, 1976.
Peterson, P. L., and Walberg, H. J. *Research on Teaching.* Berkeley, Calif.: McCutckan Publishing, 1979.
Rogers, C. R. *Freedom to Learn.* Columbus, Ohio: Charles E. Merrill, 1969.
Walker, J. E., and Shea, T. M. *Behavior Modification: A Practical Approach for Educators.* St. Louis: C. V. Mosby Company, 1976.

ENDNOTES FOR CHAPTER 5

1. See endnote 3 of Chapter 1.
2. C. R. Rogers, "The Characteristics of a Helping Relationship." *Personnel and Guidance Journal* 37 (1958): 6-16.
3. See endnote 4 of Chapter 4.
4. A.S.C.D, *Removing Barriers to Humaneness in the High School* (Alexandria, Va.: Association for Supervision and Curriculum Development, 1971). D. V. Johnson, and R. T. Johnson, *Learning Together and Alone* (Englewood Cliffs, N.J.: Prentice Hall, 1975). W. W. Purkey, *Inviting School Success. A Self Concept Approach to Teaching and Learning* (Belmont, Calif.: Wadsworth Publishing, 1978).
5. E. Hunter, *Encounter in the Classroom* (New York: Holt, Rinehart and Winston, 1972). C. G. Kemp, *Perspective on the Group Process* (Boston: Houghton, Mifflin, 1970). R. A. Schmuck, and P. A. Schmuck, *Group Processes in the Classroom.* (Dubuque, Iowa: William C. Brown, 1971).
6.   **On Humanistic Education**

    (See General References for Chapter 7.)

    On Individualizing Instruction

    Hawley, R. C., and Hawley, I. L. *A Handbook of Personal Growth Activities for Classroom Use* (Princeton, N.J.: Education Research Associates, 1972).

Jeter, J. *Approaches to Individualized Instruction*
(Alexandria, Va.: Association for Supervision and Curriculum Development, 1980).

Weisgerber, R. A. *Perspectives in Individualized Learning*
(Chicago: Peacock Publishers, 1971).

On Values

A.S.C.D. *Feeling, Valuing and The Art of Growing*
(Alexandria, Va.: Association for Supervision and Curriculum Development, 1977).

Howe, L. W., and Howe, M. M. *Personalizing Education:
Values Clarification and Beyond* (New York: Hart Publishing, 1975).

Simon, S. B.; Howe, L. W.; and Keischenbaum, H. *Values
Clarification: A Handbook of Practical Strategies for
Teachers and Students* (New York: Hart Publishing, 1972).

On Self-Directed Learning

Della-Dora, D., and Blanchard, L. J., eds. *Moving Toward
Self-Directed Learning* (Alexandria, Va.: Association for
Supervision and Curriculum Development, 1979).

Knowles, M. *Self Directed Learning. A Guide for Learners
and Teachers* (New York: Association Press, 1975).

Thatcher, D. A. *Teaching, Loving and Self Directed Learning* (Santa Monica, Calif.: Goodyear, 1973).

Wells, J. D. "Independent Study." In *Common Learnings:
Core and Interdisciplinary Team Approaches*, ed. G. Vars.
(Scranton, Penn.: International Textbook, 1969).

7. A fascinating approach to curriculum building from student needs has
been developed by Rick Little of Quest, Inc., 2207 N. Main Street,
Findlay, Ohio, 45840. See, also, H. Kirschenbaum, and B. Glaser,
Skills for Living (Findlay, Ohio: Quest, Inc., 1978).

8. F. Richards, et al., *When Students Grow* (Carrollton, Ga.: Founda-
tion for Person-Centered Projects and Research, 1977).

GENERAL REFERENCES FOR CHAPTER 5

A.S.C.D. *Perceiving, Behaving, Becoming: A New Focus for Education.*
Alexandria, Va.: 1962 Yearbook Association for Supervision and Curriculum Development, 1962.

Brophy, J. E., and Good, T. L. *Teacher-Student Relationships: Causes and Consequences.* New York: Holt, Rinehart and Winston, 1974.

Brown, G. I. *The Live Classroom.* New York: Viking Press, 1975.

Frazier, A. *Adventuring, Mastering, Associating: New Strategies for Teaching Children.* Alexandria, Va.: Association for Supervision and Curriculum Development, 1976.

Silberman, M. L. *Real Learning: A Sourcebook for Teachers.* Boston:' Little Brown, 1976.

ENDNOTES FOR CHAPTER 6

1. A.S.C.D., *Perceiving, Behaving, Becoming: A New Focus for Education* (Alexandria, Va.: 1962 Yearbook Association for Supervision and Curriculum Development, 1962).

2. A. H. Maslow, *Motivation and Personality* (New York: Harper & Row, 1970). C. R. Rogers, *Carl Rogers on Personal Power: Inner Strength and Its Revolutionary Impact* (New York: Dell Publishing, 1977). C. R. Rogers, "Toward Becoming a Fully Functioning Person," in *Perceiving, Behaving, Becoming: A New Focus for Education* (Alexandria, Va.: Association for Supervision and Curriculum Development, 1962).

3. A. W. Combs, D. L. Avila, and W. W. Purkey, *Helping Relationships: Basic Concepts for the Helping Professions* (Boston: Allyn and Bacon, 1978). A. W. Combs, F. Richards, and A. C. Richards, *Perceptual Psychology: A Humanistic Approach to the Study of Persons* (New York: Harper & Row, 1976).

4. W. H. Fitts, ed. *The Self Concept and Self Actualization* (Nashville, Tenn.: Dede Wallace Center, 1971). S. M. Jourard, and T. Landsman, *Healthy Personality: An Approach from the Humanistic Psychology* (New York: Macmillan, 1980).

5. J. H. Craig, and M. Craig, *Synergic Power: Beyond Domination and Permissiveness* (Berkeley, Calif.: ProActive Press, 1974).

6. A. W. Combs, "Human Rights and Student Rights," *Educational Leadership* 31 (1974): 672-676.

7. H. P. Constans, *Fit For Freedom* (Washington, D.C.: University Press of America, 1980).

8. J. Canfield, and H. E. Wells, *100 Ways to Enhance Self Concept in the Classroom* (Englewood Cliffs, N.J.: Prentice-Hall, 1976).

GENERAL REFERENCES FOR CHAPTER 6

Bailey, S. *The Purposes of Education.* Bloomington, Ind.: Phi Delta
    Kappa, 1976.
Kohlberg, L. "Education for Justice." In *Moral Education.* Cambridge,
    Mass.: Harvard University Press, 1970.
Sears, P. S., and Sherman, V. S. *In Pursuit of Self Esteem.* Wadsworth,
    Belmont, Calif.: Wadsworth Publishing, 1964.
Smith, V.; Bass, R.; and Burke, D. *Alternatives in Education.* Blooming-
    ton, Ind.: Phi Delta Kappa, 1976.
Tyler, R. W., ed. *From Youth to Constructive Adult Life: The Role of the
    School.* Berkeley, Calif.: McCutchan Publishing, 1978.

ENDNOTES FOR CHAPTER 7

1. Much of this chapter is adapted from two articles by the author which
   appeared in the *Phi Delta Kappan.* A. W. Combs, "What the Future
   Requires of Education," *Phi Delta Kappan,* 1981; and A. W. Combs,
   "Humanistic Education: Too Tender for a Tough World?" *Phi Delta
   Kappan,* in press, 1981.
2. A. T. Toffler, ed. *Learning for Tomorrow: The Role of the Future in
   Education* (New York: Vintage Books, 1974).
3. W. Harmin, *An Incomplete Guide to the Future* (San Francisco: San
   Francisco Book Co., 1976).
4. J. Newman, ed., *1994: The World of Tomorrow* (Washington, D.C.:
   U.S. News and World Report, 1973).
5. G. Weinstein, and M. Fontini, *Toward Humanistic Education: A Curriculum of Affect* (New York: Proeger Publishers, 1970).
6. R. H. Usher, and J. Hanke, "The 'Third Force' in Psychology and
   College Teacher Effectiveness at the University of Northern
   Colorado," *Colorado Journal of Educational Research 10 (1971):
   2-10.*
7. A.S.C.D., *Humanistic Education: Objectives and Assessment*
   (Alexandria, Va.: Association for Supervision and Curriculum Development, 1978).
8. A.S.C.D., *Humanizing the Secondary School* (Alexandria, Va.:
   Association for Supervision and Curriculum Development, 1969).
   A.S.C.D., *Removing Barriers to Humaneness in the High School*
   (Alexandria, Va.: Association for Supervision and Curriculum Development, 1971). D. H. Clark, and A. L. Kadis, *Humanistic Teaching* (Columbus, Ohio: Charles Merrill, 1971).

GENERAL REFERENCES FOR CHAPTER 7

A.S.C.D. *Humanizing Education: The Person in the Process.* Alexandria, Va.: Association for Supervision and Curriculum Development, 1967.

Glines, D. *Educational Futures IV Updating and Overlooking.* Millville, Minn.: Anvil Press, 1979.

Read, A. A., and Simon, S. B. *Humanistic Education Sourcebook.* Englewood Cliffs, N.J.: Prentice Hall, 1975.

World Future Society. *An Introduction to the study of the Future* Washington, D.C.: World Future Society, 1977.

Worth Commission on Educational Planning. *A Future of Choices: A Choice of Futures.* Edmonton, Alberta: Hurtig, 1972.

ENDNOTES FOR CHAPTER 8

1. J. L. Trump, and W. Georgiades, *How To Change Your School* (Reston, Va.: National Association of Secondary School Principals, 1978).
2. W. S. MacDonald, *Battle in the Classroom: Innovations in Classroom Techniques* (Scranton, Penn.: Intext Educational Publishers, 1971).
3. J. M. Palardy, ed., *Teaching Today: Tasks and Challenges* (New York: Macmillan, 1975).
4. A. W. Combs, R. A. Blume, A. J. Newman, and H. L. Wass, *The Professional Education of Teachers: A Humanistic Approach to Teacher Preparation* (Boston: Allyn and Bacon, 1974).

GENERAL REFERENCES FOR CHAPTER 8

Brammer, L. *The Helping Relationship: Process and Skills.* Englewood Cliffs, N.J.: Prentice Hall, 1973.

Combs, A. W. *Myths in Education.* Boston; Allyn and Bacon, 1979.

Hill, J. E. *The Educational Sciences.* Bloomfield Hills, Mich.: Oakland Community College, 1976.

NASSP. *Twenty-Five Action Learning Schools.* Reston, Va.: National Association of Secondary School Principals, 1974.

ENDNOTES FOR CHAPTER 9

1. P. W. Jackson, *Life in Classrooms* (New York: Holt, Rinehart and Winston, 1968).
2. See endnote 3 of Chapter 1.
3. Ibid.
4. V. Raimy, *Misunderstandings of the Self* (San Francisco: Jossey-Bass, 1975).
5. See endnote 4 of Chapter 1.
6. A. W. Combs, *Educational Accountability: Beyond Behavioral Objectives* (Alexandria, Va.: Association for Supervision and Curriculum Development, 1973). I. D. Welch, F. Richards, and A. C. Richards, *Educational Accountability: A Humanistic Perspective* (Fort Collins, Col.: Shields Publishing, 1973).
7. J. Goodlad, "Schools Can Make a Difference," *Educational Leadership* 33 (1975): 108-117.

GENERAL REFERENCES FOR CHAPTER 9

Rogers, C. R. *Carl Rogers on Personal Power: Inner Strength and Its Revolutionary Impact.* New York: Dell Publishing, 1977.

Index

About the Author

Arthur W. Combs received his Ph.D. in Psychology from Ohio State University. The many facets of his distinguished career have included positions as a public school teacher, school psychologist, head of a psychological clinic and counseling service, Chairman of a Department of Educational Foundations, and director of a Center for Humanistic Education. Presently he is Distinguished Professor at the University of Northern Colorado.

He has been president of the Association for Supervision and Curriculum Development and editor of its yearbook, *Perceiving, Behaving, Becoming*. He is a recipient of the John Dewey Society Award for Distinguished Service to Contemporary Education and the Teacher-Scholar of the Year Award.

His writings in education and psychology are extensive, including eighteen books and over 130 articles. Among his works are *Myths in Education: Beliefs that Hinder Progress and their Alternatives, Helping Relationships: Basic Concepts for the Helping Professions II, The Helping Relationship Sourcebook II,* and *The Professional Education of Teachers: A Humanistic Approach to Teacher Preparation II,* all published by Allyn and Bacon, Inc.